F-80 Shooting Star

in detail & scale

by Bert Kinzey
art by Rock Roszak

TABLE OF CONTENTS

CONTRIBUTORS AND SOURCES

Dana Bell

David Menard

Baird Martin

National Museum of the U. S. Air Force

Museum of Aviation, Warner Robins, Georgia

U. S. Air Force

Gerald Balzer

John Noack

Gil Hodges

Scott Manning

Jim Sullivan

Stan Parker

U. S. Air Force Armament Museum

National Naval Aviation Museum

Jim Escalle

Matthew Flegal

Paul Boyer

ISBN: 979-8-3321082-4-2

THIS BOOK IS DEDICATED TO BAIRD MARTIN

In 1952, 1Lt. Baird Martin flew combat missions in F-80C Shooting Stars
with the 80th Fighter Bomber Squadron of the 8th Fighter Bomber Group
from Suwon Air Base during the Korean War.
(Artwork by Rock Roszak)

Martin received his USAF commission upon graduation from Virginia Tech in the Class of 1950.
As a cadet at Virginia Tech, he was a member of the regimental band, the Highty-Tighties.
As an alumnus, he was a respected and honored friend of both the author and the illustrator.

Front Cover Photo: An F-80C of the 80th Fighter Bomber Squadron of the 8th Fighter Bomber Group taxis on a ramp of pierced steel planking as it heads to the runway at Suwon Air Base for a mission against communist targets. Two 1,000-pound bombs are loaded under the wings. (NMUSAF)

Rear Cover Photo: Details on the instrument panel of an F-80C are revealed in this photograph. Additional photos taken in the cockpit of this F-80C are included in the Cockpit Details section of the Shooting Star Details chapter. (Kinzey)

INTRODUCTION

Lockheed's F-80 Shooting Star was historically important as the first jet fighter to reach operational status with the U. S. Army Air Forces, which became the U. S. Air Force in 1947. It served as a fighter-bomber and a photographic reconnaissance aircraft during the Korean War. Here an F-80C of the 80th Fighter Bomber Squadron is armed with two 500-pound bombs, four 5-inch rockets, and its six .50-caliber machine guns as it awaits its next mission against communist targets. (G. Balzer Collection)

Designed under great secrecy and in considerable haste by a team led by Clarence L. "Kelly" Johnson during World War II, Lockheed's P-80 Shooting Star will forever hold a significant place in the history of American military aviation as the first jet fighter to reach operational status with the U. S. Army Air Forces. The USAAF later became the U. S. Air Force in 1947, and with the creation of the U. S. Air Force, the Shooting Star was redesignated the F-80. It would go on to serve as a fighter-bomber in the Korean War. It would become the first USAF jet fighter to score an aerial victory, and one would be credited with the first jet-on-jet aerial kill in history. RF-80s would become the first jet-powered photographic reconnaissance aircraft to serve with the USAF.

This publication provides a comprehensive look at this important jet fighter, beginning with a history chapter that traces its inception during World War II through its use in the Korean War and later service with Air National Guard squadrons. This is followed by a chapter that takes a closer look at each of the different variants of the Shooting Star, from the XP-80 prototype through the QF-80 drones and DF-80 drone directors. Because the P-80/F-80 was the first jet fighter to become operational with the Air Force, quite a few were used for various developmental experiments and tests, and these are covered in the variants chapter. The Navy's and Marine's use of the Shooting Star as the TO-1 and TV-1 is also included in that chapter.

The next chapter takes a look at the Shooting Star's combat service in the Korean War, both as a fighter-bomber and as a tactical reconnaissance aircraft. But the primary focus of all volumes in the Detail & Scale Series of publications is to illustrate the aircraft in extensive detail, and the Shooting Star Details chapter provides the most detailed look at the F-80 and RF-80 that has ever been published. More than 125 photographs and illustrations show the Shooting Star in incredible detail, both inside and out. Photographs from the files of Lockheed and the U. S. Air Force are included along with dozens taken of existing aircraft by the author and several other aviation photographers.

As with all titles in the Detail & Scale Series, this book concludes with a Modelers Section that reviews all of the scale model kits that have been produced of the Shooting Star. All kits in the standard modeling scales, from 1/144th scale through 1/32nd scale, are covered. Recommendations are made as to which kit is the best in each scale, and suggestions are made as to how to improve each kit. Master modelers Paul Boyer, Gil Hodges, and Stan Parker made important contributions to the Modelers Section.

The extensive coverage provided in this publication would not have been possible without the generous assistance of numerous contributors and sources, which are listed on the previous page. Special thanks go to the U. S. Air Force Armament Museum and the Robins Museum of Aviation for allowing the author to do detailed photography of their Shooting Stars. Additional photography was done at the National Museum of the U. S. Air Force by the author and John Noack, and Scott Manning took detail photographs of the F-80A at the Planes of Fame Museum in California. Dana Bell and Gerald Balzer contributed numerous photographs from their extensive collections. Many historical and detail photographs were obtained from the Research Division at the National Museum of the U. S. Air Force. Detail & Scale expresses a sincere word of thanks to these contributors and sources, and to all listed on the previous page. In the variants and Korean War chapters, photographs are supplemented by profile artwork created specifically for this publication by Rock Roszak.

Because the Shooting Star was initially designated the P-80, which was changed to F-80 in 1948, the use of designations in this publication will be the one in use at the time the point in the text is being discussed or the time at which a photograph being described was taken.

SHOOTING STAR HISTORY

The major design features of the P-80/F-80 Shooting Star are illustrated in this photograph of P-80A, S/N 44-85231, as it undergoes an engine change. The internal armament and radio gear were located inside a bay in the nose section with large panels on each side that provided access in much the same way Kelly Johnson had designed the nose section of the P-38 Lightning. The J33 jet engine was accessed by removing the entire tail section from the fuselage. The cockpit was covered by a three-section windscreen and a bubble canopy that provided excellent all-around visibility for the pilot. The wings and tail surfaces were straight with a conventional airfoil design. Overall, the Shooting Star was a very straight forward and simple design, and this helped speed its development. (Bell Collection)

Prior to and during World War II, Germany conducted a significant amount of research into the use of gas turbine engines to power military aircraft. Additionally, they explored the aerodynamics that would allow aircraft to fully benefit from the higher performance these new engines would be able to produce. Although several jet aircraft were flown by the Germans in World War II, primarily experimentally, the most significant was the Me 262 which became the first jet fighter to reach operational status. Powered by two axial-flow turbojet engines mounted under the wings, the Me 262 had performance that exceeded even the best propeller-driven fighters of the war.

Great Britain also produced the Gloster Meteor which became the only Allied jet fighter to reach fully operational status during World War II. It was powered by two Rolls Royce Welland centrifugal-flow jet engines mounted in the wings. Meteors entered service with the Royal Air Force's Number 616 Squadron, with the first missions being flown in late July 1944. Initially, they were used to counter the threat of German V-1 Buzz Bombs.

The United States was also working on turbojet propulsion during the war, but lagged far behind the Germans and the British. Bell Aircraft developed the XP-59 Airacomet, but it had a top speed of only 389 miles-per-hour, and in a fly-off-against a P-47D Thunderbolt and a P-38J Lightning, it had proven to be inferior to both propeller-driven fighters. As a result, following three XP-59A prototypes and thirteen YP-59A pre-production aircraft, only fifty P-59As and P-59Bs were built, and they were only used as test aircraft and as trainers.

In May 1943, when the urgency for the development of a jet fighter that could match the Me 262 and Gloster Meteor became apparent to the commander of the U. S. Army Air Forces, General Henry H. "Hap" Arnold, he called on Clarence L. "Kelly" Johnson at Lockheed to quickly design and produce the prototype for what would become America's first operational jet fighter. Johnson had previously designed the radically different P-38 Lightning, an aircraft that far exceeded other fighters in performance when it became operational, and he had a reputation as being America's top aeronautical engineer. General Arnold specified that the new aircraft had to be designed, built, and delivered to the USAAF within 150 days of the contract being signed. This seemed like an impossible task, but Johnson said he could do it if given full control of the project.

Working with his hand-picked team in a building located in a secluded area at Lockheed, Johnson designed the aircraft, got the mockup approved, and had the prototype, designated the XP-80, built by hand and ready for delivery in 143 days, beating the 150-day deadline. This feat was accomplished in large part by keeping the design simple and using proven features as much as possible. The biggest issue was the engine that was to be mounted in the fuselage. There were no jet engines in the United States that could power the aircraft, so the Americans turned to the British to obtain a Halford H-1 powerplant.

After the engine arrived on November 2, 1943, it was

Under the direction of Kelly Johnson (in the overcoat and hat just in front of the nose), workers perform checks on the XP-80 prototype shortly before its first flight. In its original configuration, the tips of the wings and the vertical and horizontal tails were blunt. However, these were later changed to rounded tips. Because it was painted in a green over gray camouflage scheme, the aircraft, nicknamed Lulu Belle, also became known as the Green Hornet. (G. Balzer Collection)

installed in the XP-80, and the aircraft was moved to Muroc Army Air Field, California. But during a ground run-up test of the engine, the air inlets collapsed, and the debris that was sucked into the engine destroyed it. The Americans urgently appealed to the British to send a replacement engine that had been intended for use in the de Havilland Vampire prototype. At that time, it was the only other H-1 engine in existence.

As the team waited for the second engine, the inlets were rebuilt and strengthened. On December 28th, the second engine arrived from England, and after it was installed and tested, the XP-80 was readied for its maiden flight. This took place on January 8, 1944, with Lockheed's chief test pilot, Milo Burcham, at the controls. Shortly after takeoff, Burcham brought the XP-80 back down, because he could not get the landing gear to retract. Once this issue was solved, he again took the prototype, by now named Lulu Belle but also called the Green Hornet because of its paint scheme, back into the air for a successful first flight. When he returned, he told Kelly Johnson that he was very pleased with the aircraft and its performance.

Flight testing of the XP-80 continued, and some changes were made along the way. Most noticeable was that the original blunt tips of the wings and tail surfaces were changed to a rounded design. During the flight tests, Lulu Belle became the first American aircraft to exceed 500 miles-per-hour in level flight.

The XP-80 was followed by two XP-80A prototypes. This was the first of two interim steps to move from the purely experimental design of the XP-80 to a combat-ready production aircraft. The XP-80As were larger than the XP-80 in both length and wingspan. The height of the vertical tail was also increased. The XP-80As were powered by a General Electric I-40 engine that was considerably more powerful than the Halford H-1, and this was necessary because they were almost 5,000 pounds heavier than Lulu Belle. This increase in weight was due to the larger airframe, a greater internal fuel capacity, and added systems and equipment. The first of the two XP-80As was delivered in a Pearl Gray paint scheme and became known as the Gray Ghost. The second had an un-

Painted in an overall Pearl Gray scheme, and known as the Gray Ghost, the first of the two XP-80As flies over the Muroc test facility in June 1944. The rounded tips on the tail and wing surfaces are apparent. (NMUSAF)

The thirteen YP-80As were produced at Lockheed right next to the production line for P-38L fighters during World War II. Deliveries of the YP-80As began in September 1944. (G. Balzer Collection)

painted natural metal finish and was named the Silver Ghost. It was used primarily for engine tests, and it had a cramped second cockpit behind the pilot's seat for a flight engineer who made notes during the test flights.

In September 1944, as the two XP-80As continued the flight test program, thirteen YP-80A pre-production aircraft began to move down an assembly line at Lockheed, parallel to a P-38L line producing Lightnings for the war effort. The flight test program began to ramp up with the additional aircraft, and after the maiden flight of the first YP-80A, it was sent to NACA for continued flight testing and wind tunnel evaluation. The second YP-80A was fitted with camera mountings in the nose to begin the development of a photographic reconnaissance variant. It was redesignated the XF-14-LO. Seven of the remaining eleven YP-80As were used in dedicated test programs to evaluate and develop the various systems of the aircraft and to continue flight testing. Four were sent to theaters of operation with two going to England and the other two to Italy in the

Mediterranean Theater. But shortly after arriving in England, one of those two YP-80As crashed, killing the pilot. The two that went to Italy flew two visual reconnaissance missions but saw no combat. They would be the only two American jet aircraft to participate in the war in any manner.

Even before World War II had ended, the first production block of P-80A-1-LOs was rolling off the assembly lines. Initially, they were painted in an overall Pearl Gray scheme. The joints between panels and the fasteners and rivets were filled with putty to make the skin as smooth as possible. These P-80As were powered by the J33-A-9 engine, the production version of the I-40 used in the XP-80As and YP-80As. It was produced by the Allison Division of General Electric.

Although the production line was running smoothly, all was not well with the program. The third YP-80A was lost in a crash due to engine failure on October 20, 1944, killing Lockheed Chief Test Pilot Milo Burcham. On March 20, 1945, the first XP-80A suffered an engine failure in flight, and flying pieces of the disintegrating engine caused significant fuselage damage resulting in the entire tail section being severed from the fuselage. Test pilot Tony LaVier managed to bail out and survive, although he injured his back and could not fly again for several months. On July 1, 1945, a production P-80A was destroyed in a fatal crash. The second YP-80A, that had been converted to the XF-14 photo recon experimental version, also crashed. On August 2, YP-80A, S/N 44-83029, crashed, then, four days later on August 6, America's leading ace and Medal of Honor recipient, Richard Bong, was killed in an accident while flying an early production P-80A. An investigation determined that this was due to a fuel pump failure, but pilot error contributed to the crash, because Bong had failed to turn on the backup electrically-operated fuel pump. By then, the total number of crashes and accidents by Shooting Stars totaled fifteen. In these, eight aircraft had been destroyed, and six pilots had been killed.

Following Bong's crash, the USAAF made the decision to ground the P-80As. On September 1 a partial lifting of the ban was made, but flying was limited only to service tests, and strict limitations were placed on maneuvering. No operational flying was permitted. Only after these service test flights were completed with no further problems was the grounding

Two of the YP-80As were sent to Italy where they flew two visual reconnaissance missions very late in World War II. They are seen here flying past Mt. Vesuvius. Neither of these Shooting Stars engaged in any combat, and they were the only American jet aircraft to see any service during the war. (G. Balzer Collection)

finally lifted and deliveries to operational units resumed. By then World War II had come to an end, and the contract for P-80A production was reduced by 2,500 aircraft. Additionally, a contract to North American to build Shooting Stars under the P-80N designation was canceled in its entirety.

As the partial restriction was lifted on September 1, the Shooting Star was finally revealed to the public. Once the service tests were completed, the USAAF wanted to begin showing off its new jet fighter, and plans were made to set a coast-to-coast speed record and regain the absolute world speed record for the United States.

The attempt to break the transcontinental speed record took place on January 26, 1946, and involved three P-80As. The flight was from Long Beach, California, to LaGuardia Field, New York. Colonel William Councill flew S/N 44-85123, and his aircraft was fitted with special external tanks under the wing tips, each of which contained 310 gallons of fuel, so that he could fly the entire distance unrefueled. The other two P-80As, S/Ns 44-85113 and 44-85121, flown by Captain Martin Smith and Captain John Babel respectively, were fitted with standard 165-gallon external tanks, and they were scheduled to make a refueling stop at Topeka Army Base during the flight. All three aircraft had their guns and ammunition boxes removed, and these were replaced with a 95-gallon fuel tank. Each of the Shooting Stars had an increased oxygen supply for the flight, as well as other modifications.

Colonel Councill took off first, and after burning all of the fuel in his external tanks, he dropped them and continued on to LaGuardia. He completed the flight and established a new transcontinental record of four hours, thirteen minutes, and twenty-six seconds with an average speed of 584.82 miles-per-hour.

Captains Smith and Babel followed. The crews at Topeka were ready and waiting with special refueling equipment and fueled the two P-80As in record time. Captain Smith completed the trip in four hours, twenty-three minutes, and fifty-four seconds, and Captain Babel's flight took four hours, thirty-three minutes, and twenty-five seconds.

Project Comet followed in May 1946 with the first mass flight across the United States by jet aircraft when P-80As of the 412th Fighter Group made the transcontinental flight from California to Washington, D.C.

P-80As are being parked outside the Lockheed plant as they come off the production lines. These aircraft were painted in the overall Pearl Gray scheme and were delivered without tip tanks. Covers are on the canopies, and many of the panels are sealed with tape to prevent moisture from getting into the aircraft. (Bell Collection)

The 1946 National Air Races at Cleveland, Ohio, were held in August. The Thompson Trophy Race for the Jet Division was won by Major Gus Lundquist flying P-80A, S/N 44-85123, the same Shooting Star in which Colonel Councill had set the transcontinental record the previous January. This was a closed-circuit race around pylons, and Major Lundquist gained the victory by a scant three seconds over World War II ace, Major Robin Olds, who came in second. The cross-country race from Van Nuys, California, to Cleveland was won by

P-80A-1-LO, S/N 44-85123, was a two-time record setting aircraft. On January 26, 1946, it was flown by Colonel William Councill to set a new transcontinental speed record of 4 hours, 13 minutes, and 26 seconds, averaging 584.82 miles-per-hour. In August of that year, it was flown by Major Gus Lundquist to win the Thomson Trophy closed course race in the Jet Division at the National Air Races at Cleveland. The markings illustrated here are the ones used at the National Air Races. (Roszak)

One of the three P-80As that was provided to the Naval Air Test Center, and given the Bureau of Aeronautics number 29668, was used to evaluate its potential for carrier operations aboard USS FRANKLIN D. ROOSEVELT, CVB-42, in 1946. During the carrier trials, the modified P-80A made several unassisted takeoffs, catapult launches, and successful arrested recoveries. The trials were flown by Marine Corps ace, Marion Carl. (Both, G. Balzer Collection)

Colonel Leon Gray, flying FP-80A, S/N 44-85465, averaging 494.8 miles-per-hour during the flight of four hours and eight minutes. The win resulted in Colonel Gray being awarded the Bendix Trophy.

The absolute world speed record was more difficult to achieve. P-80A-1-LO, S/N 44-85200, was modified to serve as the XP-80B prototype, but after it completed that role, it was again modified to become the P-80R and named "Racey." With special modifications to the airframe and engine, Colonel Albert Boyd made four speed runs across a measured course at Muroc Dry Lake on June 19, 1947. His average speed was 623.753 miles-per-hour, and this was enough to break the existing record held by a British Gloster Meteor and return the absolute speed record to the United States after twenty-four years.

Three P-80A-1-LOs were also transferred to the Navy for tests and evaluation. The second of these, BuNo. 29668, was modified with the necessary equipment for carrier evaluations. This included a catapult bridle hook, a holdback fitting, and a retractable arresting hook. The evaluation took place aboard USS FRANKLIN D. ROOSEVELT, CVB-42, in November 1946. A tanker truck with jet fuel was loaded aboard the carrier for the trials which were flown by Marine Corps ace, Marion Carl. Carl made several unassisted takeoffs and catapult launches, along with arrested recoveries. Although the trials were basically successful, the P-80A was not considered suitable for sustained carrier operations, because its landing

gear and structure were not strong enough to endure the constant stresses of launches and recoveries aboard carriers. By then, the Navy had already begun developing jet fighters for carrier operations, and contracts had been issued for several different designs. Of these, Grumman's F9F Panther and Mc-Donnell's F2H Banshee would prove to be the most successful of the Navy's first-generation jet fighters designed for carrier operations.

As the P-80As entered service with the USAAF, initially there was a higher than usual accident rate as pilots tried to make the transition from propeller-driven aircraft to jets. But eventually the accident rate improved. Beginning in 1946, the Strategic Air Command received P-80As that equipped the 1st and 56th Fighter Groups. In July 1948, World War II ace, Colonel David Shilling, led the 56th Fighter Group on the first west-to-east crossing of the Atlantic by single-engine jet fighters in Operation Fox Able. This was in response to the Berlin Crisis when the Soviet Union blocked ground access to Berlin.

As stated above, the USAAF had committed to producing a tactical reconnaissance variant of its first jet fighter early in the program. This had begun when the second YP-80A had been modified to carry vertical cameras in its nose section and was designated the XF-14-LO. This development continued with P-80A-1-LO, S/N 44-85201, which was modified with a longer and larger nose section that could house both vertical and oblique cameras. It was redesignated the XFP-80A, and upon approval of this prototype by the USAAF, Lockheed con-

The Pearl Gray paint scheme was later abandoned, and P-80As/F-80As were usually in a natural metal finish, although some were painted silver. Another change was that the AN/ARN-6 Compass Loop Antenna with its black radome replaced the landing/taxi light on the nose, and dual lights were added to the nose gear strut. P-80A, S/N 45-8350, was photographed on October 29, 1947, at Mitchel Field, New York, after this change was made. Note that this Shooting Star, which was assigned to the 56th Fighter Group, still has the pitot probe in its original location on the leading edge of the vertical tail. (NMUSAF)

Originally designated as FP-80A-5-LOs, thirty-eight P-80A-5-LOs were converted to photographic reconnaissance aircraft with a redesigned nose that housed camera equipment. These were followed by 114 additional FP-80A-5-LOs. Piloted by Colonel Leon Gray, this FP-80-5-LO, S/N 44-85465, won the Bendix Trophy by placing first in the cross country race at the National Air Races on October 11, 1946. In 1948, the designation was changed to RF-80A. (NMUSAF)

The next production variant of the Shooting Star was the P-80B/F-80B. Improvements included an uprated engine, a thinner wing airfoil, and the addition of an ejection seat in the redesigned cockpit. An AN/ARA-8A Homing Radio was added inside the vertical tail with its antenna panels on both sides of the tail. This F-80B was assigned to the 23rd Fighter Squadron of the 36th Fighter Group. (NMUSAF)

verted thirty-eight F-80-5-LOs on order to FP-80As, and this was followed by an additional contract for 114 FP-80As. In 1948, when the U. S. Air Force changed its system of designations, the FP-80As were redesignated RF-80As. These aircraft would later provide valuable photographic intelligence during the Korean War.

The P-80B followed the P-80A on the production lines in 1947 as the second fighter variant of the Shooting Star. Most important among its improvements were a more powerful J33-A-21 engine with water/alcohol injection and a redesigned cockpit to include an ejection seat to increase pilot safety in the event he had to exit the aircraft during an inflight emergency. But only 240 P-80Bs were delivered before production changed to the P-80C, which would become the defini-

tive fighter variant of the Shooting Star. Later, many P-80Bs would be upgraded to P-80C (by then redesignated F-80C) standards.

To demonstrate the Shooting Star in Europe, the 36th Fighter Wing at Furstenfeldbruk Air Base, Germany formed the Skyblazers flight demonstration team in 1949. Initially, the team had three F-80Bs, but this was soon increased to four.

In 1948, deliveries of P-80Cs began. At about the same time, the Air Force changed its designation for fighter aircraft from P (for Pursuit) to F (for Fighter), thus redesignating the third and last fighter variant of the Shooting Star as the F-80C. A total of 798 F-80Cs were delivered, easily making it the most numerous of all F-80 variants. The most important improvement was the J33-A-23 engine, which was later updated to

The definitive fighter version of the Shooting Star was the F-80C. The most important change over the F-80B was the uprated J33-A-23 or -35 engine with water/alcohol injection. F-80C-5-LO, S/N 57-540, was assigned to the 66th Fighter Squadron of the 57th Fighter Group at Elmendorf Air Force Base, Alaska, and it is shown participating in Exercise Sweetbriar on February 16, 1950. This was a ten-day cold-weather operation during which the 66th FS flew 284 sorties consisting of 353 hours and 15 minutes of flying time while maintaining an average serviceability rate of 92.8 percent. (Bell Collection)

F-80Cs became the first USAF jet fighter to see combat in the Korean War. F-80C-10-LO, S/N 49-624, is armed with two 500-pound bombs as it sits between sand-bag revetments waiting for its next mission. The yellow flashes on its tail indicate assignment to the 80th Fighter Bomber Squadron of the 8th Fighter Bomber Wing. The yellow marking on the nose indicates that this Shooting Star, named "Patricia," was formerly assigned to the 8th Fighter Bomber Squadron of the 49th Fighter Bomber Group. (NMUSAF)

the J33-A-35. The capability to carry external stores was also increased.

As deliveries continued, F-80Cs began replacing all of the F-80As and F-80Bs in active front-line squadrons, and the earlier variants were transferred to training units and Air National Guard squadrons. But those early versions usually received at least partial upgrades to F-80C standards. The 81st Fighter Group at Kirkland Air Force Base, New Mexico, and the 57th Fighter Group at Elmendorf Air Force Base Alaska, were among the units that received the F-80C in 1948.

By the time the North Koreans invaded South Korea on June 25, 1950, all fighter-bomber groups and most fighter interceptor groups in the Far East Air Force were equipped with F-80Cs. The Shooting Stars would begin playing a very important role in the war within twenty-four hours after the communists invaded. F-80Cs would score the first aerial victories by a USAF jet fighter, and the world's first jet-on-jet kill was officially credited to 1Lt. Russell Brown when he shot down a MiG-15 on November 8, 1950. But the primary missions flown by F-80Cs in Korea were fighter-bomber sorties attacking communist troops, convoys, trains, and facilities, and flying close air support missions for United Nations ground forces. The use of the Shooting Star in Korea is covered in more detail in The Shooting Star in the Korean War chapter.

Fifty F-80Cs were transferred to the Navy where they were flown as trainers for jet familiarization by Navy fighter squadron VF-52 and Marine fighter squadron VMF-311, as well as a training squadron. The Navy initially used the TO-1 designa-tion for its Shooting Stars, but this was subsequently changed to TV-1. After the two fighter squadrons received their F9F Panthers, their Shooting Stars were transferred to training units and eventually to the Naval Reserves.

As the Korean War came to an end, F-80Cs were retired from active Air Force units, but they would continue to serve in Air National Guard squadrons for several more years. Beginning in 1957, as they were replaced in the Guard units, relatively small numbers were transferred to other nations. Among these were Brazil, Chile, Columbia, Ecuador, Peru, and Uruguay. A few would remain in service into the early 1970s.

Although the F-80s and RF-80s would be retired from U. S. service before the end of the 1950s, the Shooting Star legacy would live on for many more years with the USAF, the Navy, and the Marines. The two-seat variant, initially called the TF-80C, but which was redesignated as the T-33, first flew in 1948, and it would remain in operation as a jet trainer with all three services for several decades. The Navy would take the development one step further with the T2V-1 Seastar, a carrier-capable version of the T-33 which served into the 1970s. Fitted with an afterburner and a radar for all-weather operations, the two-seat T-33 was also developed into the F-94 Starfire, a first-generation jet interceptor by the Air Force. First flown in 1949, F-94s replaced F-82 Twin Mustangs in the Air Force's all-weather fighter-interceptor groups, and a few saw limited action in Korea. But like the F-80s, The F-94s were replaced by more advanced and faster interceptors before the decade of the 1950s passed into history.

Fifty F-80Cs were transferred to the Navy and originally designated TO-1s. This designation was subsequently changed to TV-1. Most were initially assigned to one Navy fighter squadron and one Marine Fighter squadron. At least one was flown by the Naval Air Test Center. TV-1s were later flown by Navy training squadrons and by Naval Reserve units. This TV-1 was assigned to Jet Training Unit ONE (JTU-1) at NAS Pensacola, Florida, in 1949. (NNAM)

The fuselage of the P-80/F-80 was stretched in two places to make room for a second cockpit. It would become the first operational jet trainer for the U. S. Air Force, Navy, and Marines, and it would later be flown by many other nations. Originally designated the TP-80C, then the TF-80C, and finally the T-33, this trainer version of the Shooting Star would remain in active service long after all of the fighter versions were retired. They would also be built in far greater numbers. S/N 48-916 was the fourth "T-bird" off the production line, and it has the original underwing fuel tanks. (Bell Collection)

Although the Navy acquired many two-seat Shooting Stars, it was not carrier capable. To fill its needs for a jet trainer that was capable of carrier-based operations, the Navy modified the design of the T-33 to produce the T2V-1 Seastar. Although there were some noticeable differences when compared to the standard T-33, the T2V-1 clearly displayed much of the original design of the Shooting Star. (Sullivan Collection)

Another development of the design of the F-80 Shooting Star took the form of the F-94 Starfire. This was essentially a T-33 that was fitted with an afterburner and a radar in the nose so that it could perform the mission of an all-weather interceptor. F-94As and F-94Bs were armed with four 20-mm cannons in the nose, while the F-94C, with a redesigned wing airfoil and tail section, was armed exclusively with 2.75-inch rockets. This F-94B, S/N 51-5449, was assigned to the 319th Fighter Interceptor Squadron. A few F-94s saw combat during the Korean War. (Menard Collection via NMUSAF)

SHOOTING STAR VARIANTS
XP-80

The features of the sole XP-80 prototype, as it was initially completed, are revealed in this view. Originally, the tips of the wings and the vertical and horizontal tail surfaces were blunt. Note that the arrangement of the main landing gear doors was similar to that of later production aircraft, but the shapes and sizes of the doors were different. The only original markings included the national insignia in four locations, and the Lockheed logo was emblazoned on both sides of the nose and vertical tail. (NMUSAF)

When German jet fighters appeared in the skies over Europe and posed a significant threat to Allied aircraft, it was a wake-up call for General Henry "Hap" Arnold, the commanding general of the U. S. Army Air Forces. He realized that the USAAF was lagging far behind the Germans and the British when it came to jet fighter development. In May 1943, he turned to Lockheed to design and develop a capable jet fighter in record time. In response to that request, Lockheed's design for Model L-140 was submitted the following month on June 15. Two days later, the contract for $495,210 was signed, and with urgency being paramount, the aircraft was to be completed in only 150 days. In utmost secrecy, Kelly Johnson and his hand-picked team began work on what would become the XP-80.

In order to meet the very short deadline of 150 days for delivery of the prototype, Johnson kept the design very simple, using existing and proven features. Armament would be six .50-caliber machine guns mounted in the nose, and the two side panels that provided access to the weapons and radio gear would be very much like that used on Lockheed's P-38 Lightning that Johnson had also designed. The canopy was a clear bubble type like that used on late production P-47 Thunderbolts and P-51 Mustangs. Self-sealing fuel tanks and a limited amount of armor protection were included.

Aerodynamically, the design was much like that of stan-

dard propeller-driven fighters of World War II. The wings and tail surfaces were straight with conventional airfoils and blunt tips. A tricycle landing gear, similar to that on a P-39 Airacobra and P-63 Kingcobra, was included in the design. But one notable difference was that a single jet engine was to be installed inside the fuselage, and the aircraft would eventually become the first operational jet fighter with this single-engine configuration. Because of the low thrust of the early jet engines, the operational German Me 262 and the British Gloster Meteor had two engines mounted under or in the wings. The Bell P-59 Airacomet, which was an American design, but one that would never obtain operational status as a jet fighter, also had two engines mounted next to the fuselage in the wing roots.

In keeping the design simple, the XP-80 was only to be a day fighter with no radar or sophisticated instruments. The cockpit was not pressurized, and there were no trim tabs on the rudder or ailerons. The mockup was inspected on July 20, 1943, just over a month after the contract was signed.

The XP-80 had to be built entirely by hand, with workers laboring around the clock to complete the XP-80 within the specified 150 days. With the secrecy surrounding the process, the aircraft was built in a secluded building on the Lockheed grounds, and only personnel directly involved in the project were allowed near it. For quite a while, very few of the team even knew that the aircraft they were working on was a jet

Left: Lulu Belle was literally built by hand, with each part having to be made manually, then fitted on the aircraft. In spite of this, the aircraft was completed in just 143 days from the day the contract was signed. Here, a part of the skin that blends the fuselage into the left wing root is being fabricated to be fitted to the airframe. (NMUSAF)

Below: The left wing assembly, including the lowered flap, is visible in this photograph that was taken during construction of the prototype. (NMUSAF)

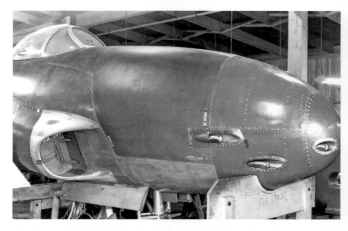

As the construction neared completion, the nose section looked like this. The aircraft was flush-riveted, and the seams were filled with putty to smooth the airflow around the aircraft and reduce drag. Although machine guns were installed, there were no ammunition boxes. Instead, instrumentation equipment for the test flights was mounted in their place. (NMUSAF)

The XP-80 was built in a building in a rather remote area on the Lockheed facility, and great secrecy was maintained. Until the engine arrived on November 2, only a very few people working on the project even knew that it was a jet aircraft. In this photograph, the original Halford H-1 engine is installed. (NMUSAF)

Taken on November 18, 1943, inside a hangar at Muroc, this photograph shows the prototype being prepared for a static engine test. It was during one of these engine tests that the two air inlets collapsed, causing damage to the engine and thus delaying the first flight of the XP-80. (NMUSAF).

fighter, and this would not become obvious to others until the jet engine arrived later to be installed.

As construction continued, the XP-80 was painted in a camouflage scheme of a medium green color (FS 595A, 34092) on the upper and vertical surfaces and medium gray (FS 595A, 36440) on the undersides. It became known as the Green Hornet, although the name Lulu Belle would be bestowed on the aircraft.

On November 2, the British Halford H-1 engine arrived and was installed in the aircraft. It was rated at 2,460 pounds of maximum thrust. Once it was installed, the XP-80 was moved to Muroc Army Air Field, California, but during a ground engine run-up test, the inlets collapsed, and the engine was damaged as pieces of the inlets were sucked into it. There was only one other H-1 engine in the world at that time, and the British obliged and sent it to Muroc as a replacement. Although this caused the first flight to be delayed, the Army accepted the completed aircraft on November 16, 143 days after the contract was signed, thus easily beating the 150-day delivery deadline. The USAAF serial number 44-83020 was assigned to the XP-80.

The replacement engine arrived on December 28, and the first flight took place on January 8, 1944, with Lockheed Chief Test Pilot Milo Burcham at the controls. After takeoff, Burcham quickly terminated the flight and landed, because he could not get the landing gear to retract. The problem was quickly fixed, and Burcham was ready to take the XP-80 into the air again

under the watchful eye of Kelly Johnson. Burcham then flew the aircraft on a much longer flight and returned with praise for its performance. During the flight test program that followed, the XP-80 became the first American aircraft to exceed 500 miles per hour in level flight.

Continued flight testing would reveal several problems, and changes were made. Most notably and obvious to the eye, the tips of the wings and tail surfaces were changed from the original blunt shape to a rounded design. The inlets were redesigned, and the incidence of the horizontal tail was increased to 1.5 degrees. A new wing fillet was added to correct stall issues, and a sensitive lateral control issue was corrected by a change in the hydraulic boost system. The fuel system was also revised.

Further service tests were flown by pilots of the 412th Fighter Group in California, beginning in November 1944. After it was replaced by the two XP-80As in the test program, Lulu Belle was used to flight test an improved version of the Halford H-1 engine which became known as the de Havilland Goblin.

After its retirement, the XP-80 was kept in storage. On May 1, 1949, ownership was transferred to the Smithsonian's National Air Museum, and it was moved to the museum's Silver Hill facility early the following year. In 1976, the decision was made to restore the aircraft, and after a restoration process that took a year and a half, it was placed on display where it remains to this day.

Above and below: The final configuration of the XP-80 is revealed in these two views. Most notable is the change to rounded tips on the wings and tail surfaces. Note the antenna mast under the nose. The prototype did not have the landing/taxi light at the top of the nose. (Both, G. Balzer Collection)

The XP-80 still exists and is part of the collection of the National Air & Space Museum where it was meticulously restored. It remains painted in its green over gray scheme. (NMUSAF)

XP-80A

The first of the two XP-80As was painted in an overall Pearl Gray scheme and was known as the Gray Ghost. The national insignia was in all four standard locations, and the Lockheed logo was applied to both sides of the nose. To identify it as the first of the two XP-80As, 01 was stenciled on both sides of the vertical tail. Three identification lights are visible near the centerline of the fuselage, just aft of the main landing gear. These would be moved to the left side on production P-80As. Note the lack of boundary layer ramps in the inlets when this photo was taken. (Bell Collection)

The sole XP-80 was followed by two additional prototypes designated XP-80As and known as Model L-141 at Lockheed. The USAAF assigned serial numbers 44-83021 and 44-83022 to the XP-80As, these being the next two serial numbers in sequence after the XP-80. The XP-80As would take the development program one step closer to creating an operational jet fighter. Several important changes were made to the design, due in part to the test flights by the XP-80, but also because of the need to bring the aircraft closer to what would become initial production standards.

The XP-80As were larger than Lulu Belle. The fuselage was lengthened from 32 feet, 10 inches to 34 feet, 6 inches, and the wingspan was increased from 37 feet to 38 feet, 10.5 inches. The weight increased significantly from 8,916 pounds to 13,780 pounds. The increase in weight was a result of the addition of more equipment, including that necessary for night flying, and a greater internal fuel capacity. The larger airframe also added to the weight. To compensate for the heavier weight, the two XP-80As were each fitted with an I-40 engine that was designed and built by the Allison Division of General Electric. It could produce 4,000 pounds of thrust, compared to the 2,460 pounds of thrust delivered by the H-1 engine that initially powered the XP-80. The improved Halford engine, later tested in the XP-80, only produced 3,000 pounds of thrust, so the I-40 offered a substantial increase in power. To provide the necessary airflow to the more powerful engine, the engine inlets were redesigned, enlarged, and they were also located a little farther aft than on the XP-80. Initially, they did not have the boundary layer plates that came later.

The first of the two XP-80As was delivered in 150 days from the signing of the contract. It was painted in an overall Pearl Gray scheme and became known as the Gray Ghost. It first flew in June 1944 with Lockheed test pilot Anthony LeVier at the controls.

Flight testing of the first XP-80A revealed a problem with high-frequency oscillations of the ailerons at high speeds called aileron buzz. This was corrected by increasing the tension on the aileron control cables. Another issue, known as inlet duct rumble, was caused by unstable boundary layer airflow inside the ducts aft of the engine inlets. To solve the duct rumble, a boundary layer ramp was added to each air inlet, thus channeling the airflow between the fuselage and the ramp through a series of vents above and below each inlet.

Another issue that had to be solved was extreme heat inside the cockpit. It was so severe that in some cases, pilots got burns on their hands when touching parts of the cockpit. A change in the cockpit pressurization and heating systems corrected this problem.

The second XP-80A was delivered without the gray paint, being left in a bare metal finish. As such, it was called the Silver Ghost. Its first flight was in August 1944. This aircraft was different from XP-80A, Number 1, in that it had a second seat installed in the cockpit for a flight engineer who would record engine information during flights. It also had a fairing that ran along the spine of the fuselage from the cockpit to the leading edge of the vertical tail. The Silver Ghost was used almost exclusively as an engine test aircraft, and it had instrumentation for that purpose.

On March 20, 1945, the Gray Ghost was destroyed in a crash. A turbine in the engine came apart, and it caused major structural damage to the aft fuselage. As a result, the entire tail of the aircraft separated from the rest of the fuselage. Tony LeVier was able to bail out of the stricken aircraft, and although he survived, he seriously injured his back when he landed on the ground. It would be several months before he would fly again. But by then, the YP-80As were flying, and the USAAF had even taken deliveries of the very first production P-80A-1-LOs, so the crash did not cause any delays in the program.

Before the age of computers, aerodynamics had to be studied in a much more conventional and rudimentary manner. Tassels of yarn were attached to the upper wing surface of the first XP-80A to study the airflow across the surface of the wing during different attitudes and flight configurations. This photo was taken during a test flight high over the Muroc test facility on December 6, 1944. (NMUSAF)

The second of the two XP-80As was originally left in a natural metal finish, and because of this, it was called the Silver Ghost. This aircraft had a second seat in the cockpit for an engineer who would make notes during engine test flights. Note the fairing that ran along the spine of the fuselage from the cockpit to the vertical tail and the scorched metal on the aft fuselage. By the time this photograph was taken, boundary layer ramps and vents had been added to the inlets to eliminate the duct rumble problem. The aircraft was later painted in the overall gray scheme, and external fuel tanks were added under the wing tips. Interestingly, this XP-80A had the straight pitot probe on the leading edge of the vertical tail and the L-shaped probe under the nose. A towel rack wire antenna was located under the aft fuselage. (Escalle Collection)

YP-80A

The first of the thirteen YP-80As, S/N 44-83023, was fitted with instrumentation probes to collect data during the flight test program. All of the YP-80A development aircraft were delivered in the Pearl Gray paint scheme. Note that the aircraft did not yet have the boundary layer ramp or the vents on the inlet. (NMUSAF)

Following the two XP-80As, thirteen pre-production aircraft were produced and designated YP-80As. Most would be used as test and development aircraft, specializing in dedicated roles or systems, but four would be sent to theaters of operation during World War II. Deliveries began in September 1944, and the production line for the YP-80As ran parallel to the P-38L Lightning production line at the Lockheed plant. The USAAF assigned serial numbers 44-83023 through 44-83035 to the YP-80As, thus continuing the series from the XP-80 and the two XP-80As that came before them.

The maiden flight of the first YP-80A was made on September 13, 1944, with Tony LeVier at the controls. This was prior to the crash of the first XP-80A when he had to bail out, injuring his back in the process as described in the previous section. The first YP-80A was then sent to the National Advisory Committee for Aeronautics (NACA) for wind tunnel and flight testing. With the USAAF already interested in developing a photographic reconnaissance version of the Shooting

Star, the second YP-80A was converted to that configuration and redesignated the XF-14. It simply had mounts for vertical cameras in the nose, rather than having the larger nose section of production photo-recon Shooting Stars that could also accommodate cameras mounted in oblique configurations. While flying as the XF-14, it was destroyed in a crash in December 1944.

Tragedy struck on October 20, 1944, when Lockheed Chief Test Pilot Milo Burcham experienced engine failure with the third YP-80A, and he was killed in the resulting crash. It was determined that the cause was due to a failure of the fuel pump, and this led to the addition of a back-up fuel pump that was electrically operated.

Among the tests conducted with the YP-80As was the use of jet-assisted takeoff units to aid in getting the aircraft into the air. Two units were attached to the underside of the fuselage and tested with success on YP-80A, S/N 44-83031. This capability was added during the production of P-80As, and it would

The YP-80As were sometimes flown with external tanks under the wing tips. However, the navigation lights remained in the forward position on each tip. Some of the YP-80As had the last two digits of their serial numbers painted on the nose. This is the twelfth of the thirteen YP-80As, S/N 44-83034. Most of the YP-80As were assigned to various test and development areas that needed to be completed before the aircraft could become operational. By the time this photograph was taken, the boundary layer ramps and vents had been added to the inlets. (NMUSAF)

YP-80A, S/N 44-83031, was used for tests with JATO bottles attached under the aft fuselage to aid in takeoff performance. This capability would later prove to be valuable in Korea during the hot summers and at bases where runways were shorter than necessary for heavily loaded Shooting Stars to take off with bombs and rockets. (Bell Collection)

Two of the YP-80As were sent to England in January 1945. The fourth YP-80A, S/N 44-83026, was one of the two shipped to England, but it was destroyed in a crash on January 28, 1945, killing the pilot, Major Frederic. A. Borsodi. Much of the wreckage from that crash is visible in this photograph. The other YP-80A, S/N 44-83027, remained in England and was used to test the Rolls-Royce B-41 engine until it too was destroyed in a forced landing due to engine failure. (NMUSAF)

remain standard on all subsequent Shooting Stars. JATO assistance for takeoffs would prove to be important in the hot summer months and on short runways during the Korean War.

In what was known as Project Extraversion, two YP-80As, S/Ns 44-83026 and 44-83027, were sent to the European Theater of Operations (ETO), and two others, S/Ns 44-83028 and 44-83029, were shipped to the Mediterranean Theater of Operations (MTO). Supporting personnel and equipment accompanied these YP-80As. The purpose was to demonstrate the capabilities of the YP-80As to USAAF units in those theaters. However, S/N 44-83026 crashed in England on January 27, 1945, killing the pilot, Major Frederic A. Borsodi. The other YP-80A that had been sent to the ETO remained in England

and was used to test the Rolls-Royce B-41 engine until it was damaged beyond repair during a forced landing on November 14, 1945, due to an engine failure.

The two YP-80As that were sent to the MTO fared much better. They were attached to the 94th Fighter Squadron of the 1st Fighter Group, a P-38 Lightning unit, and they operated out of Lesina Airfield, Italy. At that time, German jet powered Arado Ar 234 reconnaissance aircraft had begun operations in that area. But the two YP-80A flew only two visual reconnaissance missions without ever engaging in combat. This would be the only time that American jet-powered aircraft would participate in a mission of any type during World War II.

Two YP-80As, S/Ns 44-83028 and 44-83029, were sent to Italy in the Mediterranean Theater of Operations in early 1945. The two Shooting Stars flew two visual reconnaissance missions, but they did not engage in any combat. These missions represented the only time jet aircraft of the United States made any appearance during World War II. Here, S/N 44-83028 taxis across the dirt field at Lesina Airfield, Italy. (NMUSAF)

P-80A / F-80A

The first production version of the Shooting Star was the P-80A. Aircraft in the P-80A-1-LO production block were delivered in a glossy Pearl Gray paint scheme, and the seams between the panels of skin were filled with putty in an attempt to create the smoothest possible surface. The first few production aircraft were used to continue the test program. P-80A-1-LO, S/N 44-84997, was the sixth production P-80A to come off the production line. On very early P-80-1-LOs, the navigation light on the wing tip was on the leading edge. (G. Balzer Collection)

The first production Shooting Stars were originally designated P-80As, with the change to F-80A being made in 1948 after the creation of the U. S. Air Force the previous year. Three production blocks were delivered, totaling 563 aircraft:

BLOCK	AIRCRAFT	SERIAL NUMBERS
P-80A-1-LO	345	S/Ns 44-84992 – 44-85336
P-80A-5-LO	155	S/Ns 44-85337 – 44-85491
	63	S/Ns 45-8301 – 45-8363

As World War II came to an end, an additional 2,500 were canceled. Some of the first production P-80A-1-LOs were assigned to the 412th Fighter Group at Muroc Army Airfield for service tests. Three P-80A-1-LOs were transferred to the Navy and assigned Bureau numbers 29667, 29668, and 29689. Of these, 29668 was fitted with equipment for carrier operations and used for trials aboard USS FRANKLIN D. ROOSEVELT, CVB-42, in November 1946 as described in the history chapter.

Aircraft in the first block of P-80A-1-LOs were delivered in an overall Pearl Gray paint scheme. The seams between the panels forming the skin of the aircraft were filled with putty, as were the flush rivets. The paint was glossy, and all of this was to reduce the drag as much as possible. But in operational service, the putty would come off, and it was difficult to maintain the glossy surface of the aircraft for any extended period of time. This later caused the Air Force to try silver paint briefly before finally going to a natural metal finish.

Standard markings for P-80A-1-LOs in the Pearl Gray paint scheme included the U. S. national insignia on both sides of the aft fuselage, on top of the left wing, and on the bottom of the right wing. Initially, the national insignia was the one in use at the end of World War II without the red stripe in each of the rectangles, but the red stripes were added in January 1947. The buzz number, consisting of the letters PN, followed by a dash and then the last three digits of the serial number, was usually painted on both sides of the fuselage or the nose and

S/N 44-85307 was also in the first P-80A-1-LO production block, but it was near the end of that production run. It was still painted in the overall Pearl Gray scheme, but note that by this time, the navigation lights on the wings had been moved aft on the tips to the location where they would remain throughout the rest of P-80/F-80 production. By this time, large buzz numbers had appeared on the fuselage and under the left wing. Initially, Shooting Stars where assigned buzz numbers with the PN prefix, but this would later be changed to FT. (Bell Collection)

P-80A-1-LO

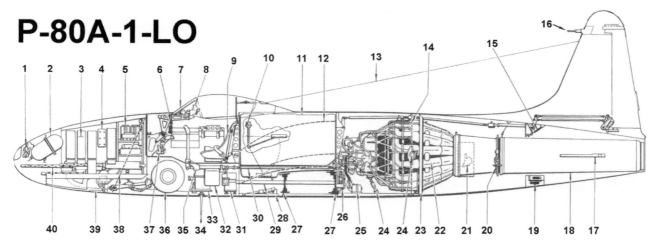

1. ADJUSTABLE LIGHT
2. OXYGEN CYLINDER
3. AMMUNITION BOX
4. ARMAMENT JUNCTION BOX
5. COMMAND RADIO
6. INSTRUMENT PANEL
7. BULLET PROOF WINDSCREEN PANEL
8. GUN SIGHT
9. PILOT'S SEAT
10. FUEL LEVEL GAGE
11. FUEL TANK
12. INTAKE AIR DUCT
13. COMMAND RADIO ANTENNA
14. FUSELAGE AFT-SECTION ATTACHING POINT
15. ELEVATOR DOWN SPRING
16. AIR SPEED PITOT
17. TAIL PIPE SUPPORT TRACK
18. TAIL PIPE
19. REMOTE COMPASS TRANSMITTER
20. TAIL PIPE CLAMP
21. ELEVATOR TAB MOTOR
22. ENGINE
23. INTAKE AIR SEAL
24. ENGINE MOUNTS
25. FUEL FILTER
26. AILERON BOOSTER UNIT
27. WING SPARS
28. DIVE RECOVERY FLAPS
29. AILERON TORQUE ROD
30. ELEVATOR PUSH-PULL ROD
31. IDENTIFICATION RADIO
32. SUB-COCKPIT JUNCTION BOX
33. BATTERY
34. IDENTIFICATION RADIO ANTENNA
35. ELEVATOR AND AILERON CONTROL ASSEMBLY
36. NOSE LANDING GEAR
37. RUDDER PEDALS
38. FUSELAGE NOSE SECTION ATTACHING POINT
39. CARTRIDGE CASE EJECTION DOORS
40. .50-CALIBER MACHINE GUNS (6)

Original features of the P-80A-1-LO are identified in this schematic. Noteworthy are the adjustable landing/taxi light in the nose, the pitot probe located on the leading edge of the vertical tail, the identification antenna mast under the left inlet, and the wire antenna for the command radio that ran from the vertical tail, through the canopy, and into the cockpit. (NMUSAF)

on the underside of the left wing. The serial number, consisting of the second digit of the two-digit year and the rest of the specific aircraft number, but without the dash, was stenciled on each side of the vertical tail.

Later, along with a change to the natural metal scheme, the prefix for the buzz number would be changed from PN to FT. With the establishment of the U. S. Air Force, the buzz number under the left wing was replaced with USAF in Insignia Blue, and the USAF marking was also applied to the top of the right wing. U. S. AIR FORCE was usually lettered above the serial number on each side of the vertical tail.

At the time the P-80A entered service, the development of ejection seats had not progressed far enough to allow the Shooting Star to be equipped with this safety device that was

clearly necessary for jet fighters. Development of the first generation of ejection seats continued, and they would become standard with the next production variant of the Shooting Star, the P-80B.

As delivered, a manually-operated canopy was installed in P-80As; however, the later electrically-operated canopy was retrofitted to many aircraft after the designation was changed to F-80A.

The General Electric I-40 engine was initially installed in the P-80A-1-LOs, but the designation was later changed to J33-GE-9A. This was subsequently upgraded to the J33-GE-11A. The P-80A-5-LOs came off the production line with the J33-GE-11A engine, but these were later upgraded to the J33-A-17. The change from GE to A in the designation was to

Some of the early P-80A-1-LOs were assigned to the 412th Fighter Group. Most had names painted on the nose. Note the smaller buzz numbers painted on the fuselage and under the left wing. The pilot's World War II scoreboard was painted on the tail. (G. Balzer Collection)

S/N 44-85464 was a P-80-5-LO, and it was the personal aircraft of Colonel David Schilling in September 1947 when he commanded the 56th Fighter Group. Colonel Shilling was an ace with the 56th FG during World War II when the group was equipped with P-47 Thunderbolts. His tally of aerial victories was painted on the left side of the fuselage of this Shooting Star. At this time, the Pearl Gray paint scheme had been discontinued, and some P-80As were painted silver instead. (Menard Collection via NMUSAF)

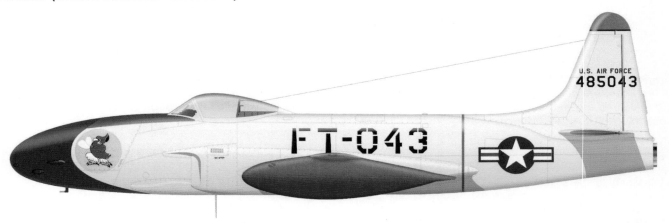

F-80A-1-LO, S/N 44-85043, was assigned to the 334th Fighter Squadron of the 4th Fighter Group in 1949. By this time, the designation had been changed from P-80A to F-80A. The pitot probe had been deleted from the leading edge of the vertical tail, and a small L-shaped probe had been added under the nose. Note that this aircraft was painted in silver lacquer, rather than being natural metal. (Roszak)

A red fuselage flash adorns an F-80A assigned to the Acrojets flight demonstration team at Williams Air Force Base, Arizona, in 1951. Note the team's T-33 in the background. (Menard Collection via NMUSAF)

Silver paint was soon discontinued on Shooting Stars, and they were left in a bare metal finish instead. Here, F-80As of the 3525th Air Gunnery Squadron are parked on the ramp at Las Vegas Air Force Base (later renamed Nellis Air Force Base) during the U. S. Air Force's first annual gunnery meet in May 1949. By this time, the prefix for the buzz numbers on F-80s had been changed from PN to FT. (Bell Collection)

Also taken in May 1949, this photograph shows F-80As of the 63rd Fighter Squadron of the 56th Fighter Group that participated in the first annual gunnery meet at Las Vegas Air Force Base. Farther down the line are F-80As of the 4th Fighter Group. (Bell Collection)

Many F-80As were later brought up to partial F-80B or F-80C standards and continued in operation with active USAF units. "STINKY" was originally produced as P-80A-5-LO, S/N 44-85440, but it is shown here after receiving most F-80C upgrades while assigned to the 9th Fighter Bomber Squadron of the 49th Fighter Bomber Group. However, it retains the original fixed pilot's seat. (Menard Collection via NMUSAF)

As later variants of the Shooting Star became available, some F-80As were assigned to training units. Here, crew chiefs walk away from three upgraded F-80As at Williams Air Force Base after completing last minute checks prior to a training mission by fledgling jet pilots. (NMUSAF)

indicate that the engine was actually produced by the Allison Division of General Electric.

Internal fuel was carried in a fuselage tank with a capacity of 207 gallons. Each wing had two fuel tanks. The smaller one, located outboard along the leading edge, carried 44 gallons, while the inboard tank in each wing had a capacity of 65 gallons. This provided a total internal fuel capacity of 425 gallons. Initially, 165-gallon external tanks could be mounted under each wing tip to supplement the internal fuel. Later, tanks with different designs and capacities were carried under the wing tips and finally on the wing tips in line with the wing rather than beneath it. These tanks are covered in the Pylons and External Stores section of the Shooting Star Details chapter.

The early P-80A-1-LOs had a clear lens at the top of the nose that covered an adjustable landing/taxi light. This would later be replaced with a radome covering the AN/ARN-6 Radio Compass Loop Antenna. When this change was made, two landing/taxi lights were mounted at the top of the nose landing gear strut.

Another change that was made with respect to exterior lighting was that the navigation lights on the wing tips were initially mounted on the leading edge of the tip, but during production of the first block of P-80A-1-LOs, the lights were redesigned and moved farther aft on the tip. P-80As also had three IFF lights mounted under the fuselage just aft of the left landing gear. These were later disconnected, and this feature was deleted on subsequent Shooting Star variants.

P-80As were delivered with the pitot probe mounted high on the leading edge of the vertical tail, but this was later deleted. Instead, an L-shaped probe was mounted under the nose. Most P-80As were retrofitted with the L-shaped probe under the nose, and the probe on the tail was deleted.

P-80As also had a wire antenna for the command radio that extended from the leading edge of the vertical tail, down through a hole in the canopy, and into the cockpit behind the pilot's seat and armor plate. This feature remained on some, but not all, P-80As/F-80As throughout their service life, even after other upgrades had been made. Another antenna on the P-80A/F-80A was a mast antenna located under the left intake for the identification radio.

As the new and more powerful variants of the engine became available, J33-A-21 engines were installed in some F-80As. This version of the engine was capable of using water/alcohol injection, but this system was made inoperable, because the F-80A did not have provisions for the associated tank for the water/alcohol solution. Otherwise, the change of engines was done with relative ease, since they were all interchangeable. Other systems were also improved. Eventually, 129 F-80A-5-LOs were upgraded to partial F-80C standards and designated F-80C-11-LOs.

As enhancements were made, the weight of the aircraft also increased. Initially, P-80A-1-LOs and P-80A-5-LOs had a maximum gross weight of 14,500 pounds. But by the time all of the upgrades had been added, the maximum gross weight had risen to 15,300 pounds.

As F-80Bs and F-80Cs replaced the F-80As in front line active USAF squadrons, many were transferred to training units, while others went to Air National Guard squadrons, the first being the California Air National Guard in 1947. In both cases, these units received F-80As that had the partial upgrades to F-80B or F-80C standards. Photos of these Shooting Stars often show the later style fuel tanks under the wing tips or mounted in line with the wings.

Beginning in June 1947, other upgraded F-80As were reassigned to Air National Guard units. S/N 44-85190 was flown by the Wisconsin ANG. It has the L-shaped pitot probe under the nose and the electrically operated canopy, but it retains the wire antenna for the command radio. The Shooting Star is fitted with the last style of external fuel tanks that were mounted under the wing tips. (Menard Collection via NMUSAF)

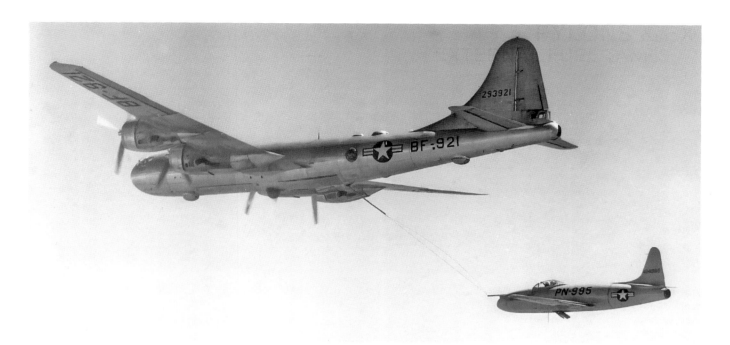

P-80As were used for a variety of experimental programs. One of the most unusual involved towing a Shooting Star by a bomber. P-80A-1-LO, S/N 44-84995, the fourth P-80A off the production line, was used for this test. It is seen here being towed by a B-29 Superfortress. The hook for the tow cable was at the end of a boom attached to the nose. Like other parasite fighter programs that followed, this experiment was abandoned. (NMUSAF)

Above and right: Another interesting experiment was to fit ramjet engines to the wing tips of a Shooting Star. S/N 44-85042 was used for this program. External fuel tanks were moved to the underwing pylons. This proved to be another short-lived experiment. (Both, NMUSAF)

25

Above: Other early P-80As were used to test different gun arrangements in the nose. One such arrangement involved mounting four .50-caliber machine guns so that they could fire upwards at bomber targets. This was derived from similar gun arrangements, known as Schrage Musik, used in some German night fighters during World War II. (NMUSAF)

Right: Another elevated gun arrangement consisted of two 20mm cannon instead of the four machine guns. In both cases, P-80A-1-LO, S/N 44-85044, was used for these tests. This Shooting Star had previously participated in the National Air Races in 1946. (NMUSAF)

Different fixed forward-firing gun arrangements were also evaluated on P-80As, involving cannon armament instead of machine guns. The primary goal was to explore means of increasing the firepower of the Shooting Star. Two of these cannon arrangements are illustrated in these photographs. (Both, NMUSAF)

Cannon armament was not the only means of increasing the firepower of Shooting Stars that was evaluated. P-80A-1-LO, S/N 44-85116, had an automatic rocket launcher installed in the nose. A launch tube extended well forward of the modified nose cone. (NMUSAF)

Above and below: Details inside the modified nose section are illustrated in these two photographs. The rockets were contained inside tubes that are displayed on the ground in the photo at right. (Both, NMUSAF)

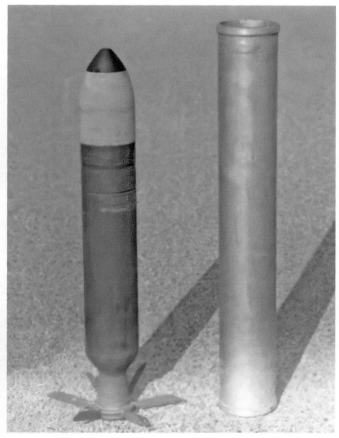

This closeup provides a good look at one of the rockets and its container tube. The rocket had six folding fins that popped out after the rocket left the launch tube on the nose. But very few rockets could be carried, and their lack of accuracy made this armament ineffective and impractical. (NMUSAF)

EF-80A

Above and below: After it was used as a test bed for the upwards-firing machine gun and cannon arrangements, as illustrated in the previous section of this chapter, P-80A-1-LO, S/N 44-85044, was modified to evaluate a pilot-prone flying position. A second cockpit was installed in the nose of the Shooting Star forward of the standard cockpit, and it was covered by a bubble canopy. In this configuration, the aircraft was redesignated as the EF-80A. (Both, NMUSAF)

XP-80B & P-80R

The record-breaking P-80R is now on display at the National Museum of the U. S. Air Force near Dayton, Ohio. It remains in the configuration it was in when it made its record-setting flight. Note the larger redesigned inlet. (Kinzey)

P-80A-1-LO, S/N 44-85200, was initially modified to serve as the prototype for the P-80B. In this configuration, it was redesignated XP-80B. After serving in this role, it was again modified in an attempt to set a closed-course speed record. In its new configuration, it was redesignated P-80R and named "Racey." The modifications included a smaller canopy, larger and redesigned air inlets, a shorter wingspan with an extended leading edge and squared off tips, and an uprated J33-A-23 engine. Additionally, all armament was removed, and all drag-producing openings were sealed to reduce drag. The flush rivets and joints between panels were filled. Gloss gray paint was applied, and then the surface was waxed.

On June, 19, 1947, Colonel Albert Boyd flew the P-80R over the measured course at Muroc Army Air Field (now Edwards Air Force Base) and set a new world's absolute speed record averaging 623.753 miles-per-hour on four runs over the closed course. This broke the record held by a British Gloster Meteor, and it returned the record to the United States after nearly twenty-four years.

Above: This closeup provides a look at the much smaller windscreen and canopy used on the F-80R. There was very little room above or to the sides of the pilot's head. (NMUSAF)

Left: Colonel Albert Boyd flies the P-80R just fifty feet above the dry lake bed at Muroc Army Air Field on one of his four passes as he sets a world speed record of 623.753 miles-per-hour. (NMUSAF)

F-80B

F-80Bs of the 71st Fighter Squadron of the 1st Fighter Wing are serviced prior to a training exercise. Note the practice bomb under the wing tip of S/N 45-8504. Another addition that was unique to the F-80B was the AN/ARA-8A Radio Homing Device with its distinctive antenna panels on each side of the vertical tail. The antenna panel is clearly visible as an off-white area on this Shooting Star. (Bell Collection)

Development of the F-80B (designated the P-80B until 1948) began when P-80A-1-LO, S/N 44-85200, was converted to the XP-80B prototype. After serving in this developmental role, it was converted to the P-80R and used to set a world speed record as covered on the previous page.

The P-80B/F-80B turned out to be an interim step between the P-80A/F-80A and the definitive variant, the F-80C. Only 240 were built before the production lines changed to the F-80C, which would be built in far greater numbers. The production blocks were:

BLOCK	AIRCRAFT	SERIAL NUMBERS
P-80B-1-LO	3	S/Ns 45-8478 – 45-8480
P-80B-5-LO	1	S/N 45-8481
P-80B-1-LO	84	S/Ns 45-8482 – 45-8565
P-80B-5-LO	30	S/Ns 45-8566 – 45-8595
P-80B-1-LO	122	S/Ns 45-8596 – 45-8717

Early production P-80Bs were delivered with the pitot probe on the leading edge of the vertical tail, but as with the P-80A, this was changed to the L-shaped probe under the nose, and earlier P-80Bs were retrofitted with the L-shaped probe. Likewise, early P-80Bs originally had the manually-operated canopy, but the electrically-operated canopy became standard during production of the P-80Bs and was also retrofitted to existing aircraft. P-80A-5-LOs had special provisions for cold weather operations, including special seals and low temperature greases.

The P-80B incorporated all of the changes and improvements that had been made during P-80A production, but more important upgrades were also added. Primary among these was a redesigned cockpit to accommodate an early ejection seat, thus significantly improving a pilot's chances of survival if he had to exit the aircraft during an inflight emergency. The other major improvement was a more powerful J33-A-21 engine with water/alcohol injection. A tank containing thirty gallons of the water/alcohol solution was added. Standard thrust remained 4,000 pounds, but during water/alcohol injection this was increased to 5,200 pounds.

Structural changes were made to increase the strength of the airframe. The armor protection was increased, and electronics systems were upgraded. The wire antenna for the command radio, which was standard on the P-80A, was deleted because wire antennas became obsolete in the higher speeds being attained by jet aircraft. An AN/ARN-6 Radio Sense antenna was embedded in the top of the canopy, and antenna panels for the AN/ARA-8A Radio Homing Device were added on each side of the tail. The AN/ARC-3 radio antenna was located in the cap at the top of the vertical tail and was known as the pick axe antenna because of its shape. A mast for the SCR-695-A radio was under the left inlet. As the newer external fuel tanks became available, these were used on the F-80Bs. Gross weight without external fuel tanks was 12,900 pounds, and with full 165-gallon tanks, the gross weight was 15,350 pounds. Interestingly, the cost of the F-80B was less than that of the previous F-80A. Each F-80B cost approximately $95,000, compared to $107,796 for an F-80A.

Internal armament remained six 50-caliber machine guns mounted in the nose with 300 rounds of ammunition for each weapon. Bombs, chemical tanks, and external fuel tanks could be carried under the wingtip stations, as they could be

F-80B

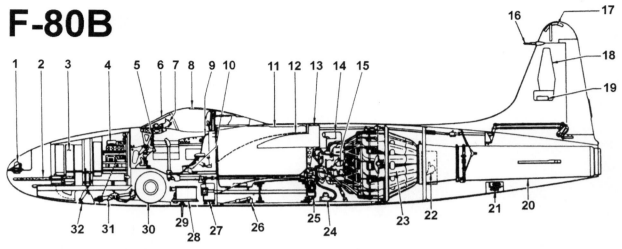

1. AN/ARN-6 RADIO COMPASS LOOP ANTENNA
2. .50-CALIBER MACHINE GUNS (6)
3. AMMUNITION BOXES (6)
4. AN/ARC-3 AND AN/ARN-6 RADIO
5. INSTRUMENT PANEL
6. BULLET PROOF WINDSCREEN PANEL
7. GUN SIGHT
8. AN/ARN-6 RADIO SENSE ANTENNA
9. PILOT'S EJECTION SEAT
10. "G" VALVE
11. FUSELAGE FUEL TANK

12. INTAKE AIR DUCT
13. WATER TANK
14. TURBO-REFRIGERATOR
15. THROTTLE
16. AIR SPEED PITOT
17. AN/ARC-3 RADIO PICK AXE ANTENNA
18. AN/ARA-8A RADIO ANTENNA
19. AN/ARA-8A RADIO HOMING DEVICE
20. TAILPIPE
21. GYROSYN COMPASS FLUX VALVE
22. ELEVATOR TAB MOTOR

23. ENGINE
24. FUEL FLOW METER
25. AILERON BOOSTER UNIT
26. DIVE RECOVERY FLAPS
27. SCR-695-A RADIO
28. BATTERY
29. SCR-695-A RADIO ANTENNA
30. NOSE LANDING GEAR
31. LANDING AND TAXI LIGHTS
32. CASE EJECTION DOOR

The features of the F-80B are identified in this schematic. Noteworthy are the pilot's ejection seat and the AN/ARA-8A Radio Homing Device with its panel antenna on the vertical tail. (NMUSAF)

on the P-80A. Although rockets were first tested on P-80Bs, the ability to employ them operationally did not become standard until the F-80C.

As with the F-80As, many F-80Bs received upgrades to partial or full F-80C standards. But as production F-80Cs became available, F-80Bs followed the F-80As into training units and Air National Guard squadrons. F-80B-1-LO, S/N 45-8557, was transferred to the U. S. Navy and assigned Bureau Number 29690. It was flown by the Navy's test facility at Point Mugu, California.

One F-80B-1-LO, S/N 45-8557, was transferred to the U. S. Navy and given the Bureau Number, 29690. It was assigned to the test facility aboard NAS Point Mugu, California. (G. Balzer Collection)

Three F-80Bs, each representing a squadron of the 36th Fighter Group based at Furstenfeldbruk Air Base, Germany, fly in formation. The blue arrow flash and tail band were for the 23rd Fighter squadron, the red flash and tail band were used by the 22nd Fighter Squadron, and the 53rd Fighter Squadron used the green flash and tail band. Again, the AN/ARA-8 antenna panels on the vertical tails are clearly visible in this photo. These were only on F-80Bs. (Bell Collection)

In 1949, the 36th Fighter Wing formed the Sky-blazers flight demonstration team to perform in USAFE. F-80B-1-LO, S/N 45-8663, was one of the Shooting Stars flown by the team that began with three F-80Bs, but soon added a fourth. The team retained the 36th Fighter Wing's arrow flash on the fuselage and fuel tanks, but they added the team's name on the nose of the aircraft. (Menard Collection via NMUSAF)

As F-80Cs became available, many F-80Bs were assigned to training units. S/N 45-8560 was an example. It is fitted with Fletcher fuel tanks under the wing tips as it awaits its next flight at Williams Air Force Base. (NMUSAF)

Other F-80Bs were reassigned to Air National Guard squadrons. Many of the Guard units used relatively simple markings on their aircraft. An example was this F-80B that was flown by the Wyoming ANG. It was fitted with one of the late external tanks that were mounted in line with the wing, rather than being suspended beneath the tip. (Roszak)

INLINE TYPE TIP TANK SHOWN SEPARATELY
TO REVEAL MARKINGS ON AFT FUSELAGE

Other Guard squadrons did add some color to their F-80Bs. One such case was the Oklahoma ANG that used blue markings on its Shooting Stars. (Roszak)

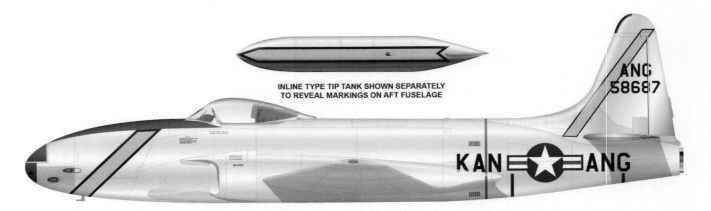

INLINE TYPE TIP TANK SHOWN SEPARATELY
TO REVEAL MARKINGS ON AFT FUSELAGE

The Kansas ANG adorned its F-80Bs with yellow markings. By the time they served with the Guard, most F-80Bs had been upgraded to F-80C standards. (Roszak)

Perhaps the most colorful of all F-80Bs flown by the Guard were those assigned to the "Minute Men" of the Colorado ANG. Extensive use of red markings was found on their Shooting Stars. (Menard Collection via NMUSAF)

Some F-80Bs assigned to Guard units were used in utility roles. This F-80B was a target tug used in aerial target practice with the Texas ANG, and it had high visibility orange painted on its upper and vertical surfaces. (NMUSAF)

F-80C

The F-80C was the definitive fighter version of the Shooting Star. This F-80C-5-LO, S/N 47-545, bears the colorful markings of Colonel John W. Mitchell, the commanding officer of the 57th Fighter Group. The red, green, and yellow markings on the nose and the stripes on the fuselage represent the colors of the three squadrons assigned to the wing. This photo was taken at the first USAF Gunnery Meet at Las Vegas Air Force Base, Nevada, in 1949. At this time, the group was assigned to the Alaskan Air Command and was based at Elmendorf Air Force Base. Accordingly, their Shooting Stars had the high visibility markings used by the Alaskan Air Command during that time period. (Menard Collection via NMUSAF)

Deliveries of the definitive variant of the Shooting Star began in 1948, just shortly before the Air Force changed the designation from P-80C to F-80C. In the F-80C, the fighter-bomber capability of the Shooting Star was enhanced, and other improvements were made. A total of 798 were delivered, easily making the F-80C the most numerous of all variants. F-80Cs were delivered in these production blocks:

BLOCK	NUMBER	SERIAL NUMBERS
F-80C-1-LO	54	S/Ns 47-171 – 47-224
	1	S/N 47-525
	4	S/Ns 47-601 – 47-604
	32	S/Ns 47-1380 – 47-1411
	21	S/Ns 48-376 – 48-396
	50	S/Ns 48-863 – 48-912
F-80C-5-LO	75	S/Ns 47-526 – 47-600
F-80C-10-LO	475	S/Ns 49-422 – 49-878
	100	S/Ns 49-1800 – 49-1899
	4	S/Ns 49-3597 – 49-3600

As with the F-80B-5-LOs, the seventy-five F-80C-5-LOs were modified with special seals and lubricants for cold weather operations. Fifty F-80Cs were transferred to the U. S. Navy and Marines and initially redesignated TO-1s. The designation was later changed to TV-1. These Shooting Stars are covered in the next section of this chapter.

The first F-80Cs off the production line had the J33-A-23 engine, but this was later upgraded to the J33-A-35. A backup electrically-driven fuel pump had been installed in all Shooting Stars after Milo Burcham had been killed in a crash of the third YP-80A, due to failure of the engine-driven fuel pump. But the electrically-driven fuel pump was deleted in the F-80C, and instead there were dual engine-driven pumps. If one failed, the other was sufficient to keep the engine operating. This eliminated the need for the pilot to switch on the electrically driven emergency fuel pump. Main and emergency controls were also installed in the fuel system. The tank for the water/alcohol fluid was increased from thirty gallons in the F-80B to fifty gallons in the F-80C. F-80Bs had been plagued with fumes getting into the cockpit when the water/alcohol injection system was used, so an actuating cylinder was installed that automatically shut off pressurizing air to the cockpit when the injection system was operating.

To increase the capabilities of the F-80C in the fighter-bomber role, a mid-wing hardpoint was added under each wing. These could be used to carry bombs up to the 1,000-pound size, fire bombs made from 75-gallon fuel tanks filled with napalm, chemical tanks, or additional external fuel tanks. The capability to carry and employ 5-inch rockets was also added to the F-80C. Originally tested on an F-80B, this capability was intended to include a maximum of eight rockets mounted in four pairs, two pairs under each wing. Although the flight manual for the F-80C illustrates the loading of eight rockets, the accompanying text states that only four could be mounted singly. Photographs of Shooting Stars armed with rockets in Korea never showed more than four being loaded. Retractable tabs were installed in the underside of each wing to mount the rockets. When not in use, they folded flush into the wing. Photos of the rockets and tabs are included in the Pylons and External Stores Details section and the Wing Details section of the Shooting Star Details chapter.

As they became available, F-80Cs quickly replaced the earlier variants in the active USAF units that were equipped

F-80C

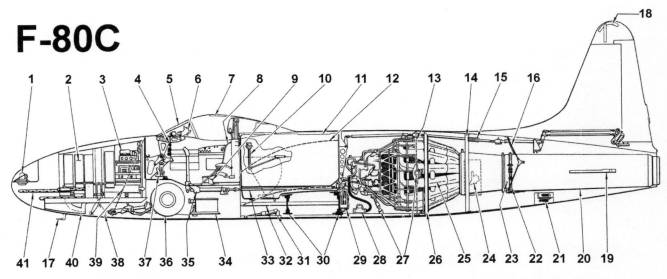

1. RADIO COMPASS LOOP ANTENNA
2. AMMUNITION BOXES (6)
   300 ROUNDS EACH
3. RADIO INSTALLATION
4. INSTRUMENT PANEL
5. BULLETPROOF WINDSHIELD PANEL
6. GUN SIGHT
7. RADIO SENSE ANTENNA
8. PILOT'S EJECTION SEAT
9. "G" VALVE
10. FUEL LEVEL GAGE
11. FUEL TANK (207 GALLONS)
12. INTAKE AIR DUCT
13. FUSELAGE AFT-SECTION ATTACHING
    POINT

14. DIAPHRAGM
15. DIAPHRAGM BELLOWS
16. TAIL PIPE SLING
17. AIR SPEED PITOT
18. RADIO PICK AXE ANTENNA
19. TAIL PIPE SUPPORT TRACK
20. TAIL PIPE
21. GYROSYN COMPASS FLUX VALVE
22. TAIL PIPE CLAMP
23. TAIL PIPE ADAPTER
24. ELEVATOR TAB MOTOR
25. ENGINE
26. INTAKE AIR SEAL
27. ENGINE MOUNTS
28. FUEL FLOW METER

29. AILERON BOOSTER UNIT
30. WING SPARS
31. DIVE RECOVERY FLAPS
32. AILERON TORQUE ROD
33. ELEVATOR PUSH-PULL ROD
34. BATTERY
35. ELEVATOR AND AILERON
    CONTROL ASSEMBLY
36. NOSE LANDING GEAR
37. RUDDER PEDALS
38. LANDING LIGHTS
39. FUSELAGE NOSE-SECTION
    ATTACHING POINT
40. CASE EJECTION DOOR
41. .50-CALIBER MACHINE GUNS (6)

Features of the F-80C are identified in this schematic. Noteworthy is the elimination of the AN/ARA-8A Homing Device and its antenna panel on the sides of the vertical tail. The mast antenna for the SCR-695-A Radio was also deleted under the forward fuselage. (NMUSAF)

with Shooting Stars. The F-80C would be the fighter-bomber variant used in the Korean War, initially equipping both fighter-bomber groups and fighter-interceptor groups that saw combat. However, by the time the armistice was signed, all F-80Cs had been retired or replaced by other types of aircraft. Information about the units that flew F-80Cs during the war can be found in The Shooting Star in the Korean War chapter.

In the post-war years, F-80Cs were quickly retired from

service with active Air Force units, being replaced in the fighter-bomber role by the F-84 Thunderjet. In the air superiority role, the F-86 Sabre became the dominant fighter in the USAF for several years. But F-80Cs would continue to serve in several Air National Guard units for a few more years. Some would be used in utility roles like towing targets. Their final service was as drones and drone controllers.

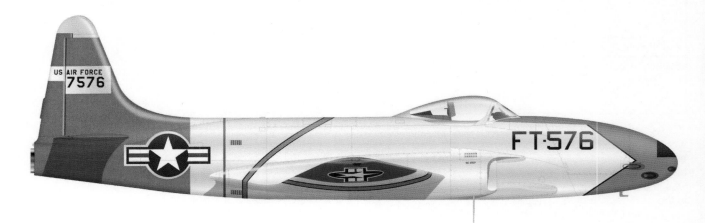

The green markings indicate that this Shooting Star was assigned to the 6th Fighter Squadron of the 57th Fighter Group. (Roszak)

The yellow flashes of the 80th FBS, used throughout most of the Korean War, are displayed on the tail of S/N 49-452. Yellow is also used to outline the black letters and numbers of the buzz number. Note that the blow-in doors on top of the fuselage are open while the engine is running at idle speed. (G. Balzer Collection)

Like the Air National Guard, active USAF units also used Shooting Stars in utility roles late in their operational service. The upper and vertical surfaces of this F-80C were painted in high visibility orange when the aircraft was used as a target tug for aerial gunnery practice. (NMUSAF)

As previously had been the case with F-80As and F-80Bs, F-80Cs were assigned to Air National Guard units as they were replaced in active Air Force squadrons. F-80C-1-LO, S/N 48-393, served with the 196th Fighter Squadron which was a unit of the California Air National Guard. The only marking that indicates the squadron assignment is the 196 FTR.SQD. lettered on the fuel tanks under the wing tips. Note that the tanks are one of the original 165-gallon designs. NG on the vertical tail identifies the Shooting Star as an Air National Guard aircraft. (NMUSAF)

TO-1 / TV-1

VF-52 flew TO-1 Shooting Stars while waiting for delivery of Grumman F9F Panthers. The use of the TO-1s permitted the pilots to get jet fighter experience before the Panthers became available. The markings used by VF-52 were simple and consisted only of an S code on the vertical tails. Eight of the squadron's TO-1s are shown flying near San Diego in 1948. Along with VF-51, VF-52 would be one of the Navy's first two F9F-2 Panther squadrons to see combat in Korea. (NNAM)

As stated in the previous section, fifty F-80Cs were transferred to the U. S. Navy and Marines in 1948. These were initially designated TO-1s by the Navy's Bureau of Aeronautics, with the T being for trainer and the O being the Navy's designation for Lockheed. However, the Navy later changed its letter designator for Lockheed to V, thus causing the designation to become TV-1. In either case, the T in the designation indicated that the Navy intended these Shooting Stars to be used only in a training role.

Although a few went to facilities, such as the Naval Air Test Center at NAS Patuxent River, Maryland, and to a dedicated training unit, twenty-five were initially sent to Navy fighter squadron VF-52 at NAS North Island, California, and sixteen were assigned to Marine Fighter Squadron VMF-311 at nearby MCAS El Toro. These two squadrons flew the TO-1s to give their pilots experience flying a jet fighter as they waited for their Grumman F9F-2 Panthers to be delivered. Although the TO-1s were not carrier capable, the early experience in jet

fighters proved to be valuable for the pilots of the two squadrons that would be among the first Navy and Marine fighter squadrons to see combat in Korea.

Once VF-52 and VMF-311 received their Panthers, their TO-1s were transferred to training units where they continued to serve in a training role until replaced with T-33s which the Navy designated TO-2s, later changing this designation to TV-2. Eventually, the T2V Seastar, a carrier-capable development of the TV-2, was added to the Navy's inventory of jet trainers.

The final service of TV-1s was in Reserve units as proficiency aircraft for Naval Reserve aviators. Throughout their service with the Navy, the TV-1s were usually left in a natural metal finish with austere markings. Typically, only a tail letter or letters identified the unit to which the aircraft was assigned. In some cases, the unit's designation was painted under the NAVY on the aft fuselage. Reserve TV-1s usually had the orange fuselage band to denote a Naval Reserve aircraft.

The only Marine squadron that flew TO-1s in 1948 was VMF-311 which received sixteen TO-1s. It identified its Shooting Stars by using the WL tail code which it would later use on its F9F Panthers. Note the Marine Corps insignia on the forward fuselage. VMF-311 would later become the first Marine land-based jet fighter squadron to see combat in Korea with their F9F-2 Panthers. (NNAM)

After VF-52 and VMF-311 received their Grumman Panthers, the TO-1s, redesignated TV-1s, were transferred to training units. These Shooting Stars display the KA tail codes used by Advanced Training Unit THREE (ATU-3) at NAS Kingsville, Texas, in 1952. (NNAM)

The final use of TV-1s by the U. S. Navy was with Reserve units. With the Reserves, the Shooting Stars usually had the orange fuselage band to indicate a Reserve aircraft. They were typically fitted with the last style of external tanks that were mounted under the wing tips. The Reserve unit at NAS Oakland, California, identified by the F tail code, flew TV-1, BuNo. 33850. TV-1s in Reserve squadrons often had two or more of their machine guns removed. (Roszak)

This TV-1 was a departure from the very simple markings usually found on the Navy's Shooting Stars. It was painted in an overall white scheme with high visibility markings while assigned to NAS Moffett Field, California. (Roszak)

F-14A, FP-80A, RF-80A, & RF-80C

The first jet powered tactical reconnaissance aircraft to enter service with the U. S. Air Force was the RF-80A. This was a rather simple and straight-forward modification that replaced the standard nose and its six .50 caliber machine guns with a longer and larger nose to house cameras and their associated equipment instead. A pilot assigned to the 160th Tactical Reconnaissance Squadron of the 117th Tactical Reconnaissance Wing at Neububerg Air Base, Germany, poses with a K-17 aerial camera in front of an RF-80A in May 1952. (Bell Collection)

With speed being the best defense for an unarmed tactical reconnaissance aircraft, the USAAF was quick to develop a photographic reconnaissance version of its first jet fighter. The urgency with which the USAAF wanted to develop a jet powered tactical reconnaissance aircraft was illustrated by the fact that the second YP-80A (just the fifth Shooting Star produced) was converted to an initial photo recon prototype and designated the XF-14. At that time, the USAAF was using F

as its designation for a photographic reconnaissance aircraft. The XF-14 retained the same nose as the other XP-80As, but mounts for two vertical cameras were installed in place of the machine guns and their armament.

The XF-14 was destroyed in a crash in December 1944, but this did not end or even slow the development of a reconnaissance variant of the Shooting Star. P-80A-1-LO, S/N 44-85201, was converted as an improved prototype and desig-

The gun sight was removed from RF-80As, and it was replaced with the control and indicator panel for the camera equipment. The installation of this panel also necessitated the rearrangement of some of the instruments and gages. (NMUSAF)

P-80A-1-LO, S/N 44-85201, was converted to serve as the prototype for the photo reconnaissance version of the Shooting Star. After the lengthened and modified nose was installed, USAAF representative, LtCol. Matos, inspected the prototype which was initially designated the XFP-80A. (NMUSAF)

The blue checkerboard markings on RF-80A, S/N 45-8408, indicate that it was assigned to the 363rd Tactical Reconnaissance Wing at Lockbourne Air Force Base, Ohio. In 1974, the base was renamed Rickenbacker AFB. (NMUSAF)

nated XFP-80A, with the F to indicate a photo reconnaissance variant being added in front of the standard P-80A designation. This conversion included a longer and larger nose section with stations for three vertical and two oblique camera mountings. This design would be continued forward to the production aircraft.

The first production reconnaissance Shooting Stars were thirty-eight P-80A-5-LOs that were converted by Lockheed with the designation FP-80A-LO. These were followed by an additional 114 that were ordered as FP-80A-5-LOs, rather than being conversions. These aircraft were assigned the serial numbers 45-8364 – 45-8477. Except for the cameras and their associated equipment in the redesigned nose and the camera controls in the cockpit, the rest of the aircraft and its systems remained the same as in the P-80A-5-LO fighters. Like the F-80As, the RF-80As lacked an ejection seat for the pilot. In 1948, when the change in designations for all Shooting Stars was made, the FP-80s were redesignated RF-80As.

The temperature in the camera compartment was controlled by a thermostat. This had to be maintained at the proper level to prevent fogging of the camera windows. The indi-

vidual cameras were controlled by switches on a panel that was added to the upper area of the instrument panel. Blinker lights on the panel indicated when the cameras were on and the film was rolling. Exposure counters indicated the number of frames that had been taken, and intervalometers were used to regulate the time interval at which the photos were taken.

RF-80As were used extensively during the Korean War, but there never seemed to be enough to meet mission demands. As a result, a number of F-80Cs were converted to RF-80Cs in Japan, but the conversions took two different forms. The simplest retained the standard F-80C nose and two of the machine guns, but vertical cameras were mounted in place of the other four guns and their ammunition magazines. In the other case, a full recon nose was installed on an F-80C airframe. Additionally, some existing RF-80As were upgraded to F-80C standards, but these did not increase the number of recon Shooting Stars that were available. In any event, the RF-80C was not actually a true production variant of the Shooting Star. They were simply changes or conversions made to existing aircraft.

RF-80A-5-LO, S/N 45-8412, was assigned to the 4th Tactical Reconnaissance Squadron. The three bands on the aft fuselage and the number 2 on the vertical tail indicate that this RF-80A was assigned to the squadron's executive officer. (NMUSAF)

Above: Five of the six camera windows as installed in RF-80As are visible in this view. There were three rectangular windows in the bottom of the nose for vertical cameras, and one small window was low on the right side of the nose for mounting an oblique camera to the right. The forward-looking camera had a small circular window in front of the nose. (NMUSAF)

Right: As an airman installs a vertical camera, the pilot of an RF-80A checks the installation through the window from below. (Bell Collection)

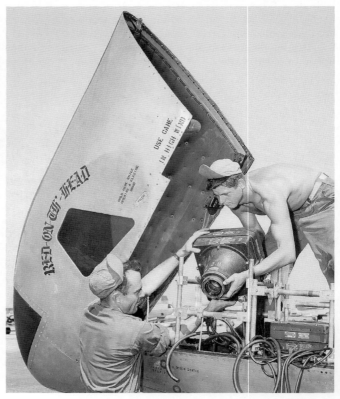

Above: Details inside the camera bay are revealed here. The framework for the camera mounts could be changed depending on the types of cameras used and how they were to be mounted. (NMUSAF)

Right: Airmen install a camera in the left oblique mount. The window for the left oblique camera was much larger and higher on the nose than the small window for the right oblique camera. Oblique cameras could be mounted simultaneously on both sides with the left camera being above the right camera. (G. Balzer Collection)

A full complement of cameras is installed in this RF-80. These include vertical cameras in all three positions as well as oblique cameras on both sides. (Both, G. Balzer Collection)

Right: RF-80A, S/N 45-8455, was assigned to the 4th Tactical Reconnaissance Squadron and named "Little Joe." The name "Patsy" was also painted in red on the external fuel tank. In this case, the tank is one of the original 165-gallon tanks. (Menard Collection via NMUSAF)

Below: RF-80A, S/N 44-85279, was named "RED FEATHER" and was assigned to the 45th Tactical Reconnaissance Squadron late in the operational service of the Shooting Star. It is fitted with the external fuel tanks that were mounted in line with the wing, rather than being under the wing tip. Because of the camera windows under the nose, the pitot probe remained high on the leading edge of the vertical tail on RF-80As. (G. Balzer Collection)

DF-80A DRONE DIRECTORS & QF-80 DRONES

Following their operational service with active USAF and Air National Guard Units, many Shooting Stars were convert-ed to DF-80 drone directors and QF-80 target drones. In either case, these aircraft were usually painted in an overall high visibility International Orange scheme. A Q was added in front of the buzz number on the fuselage aft of the na-tional insignia for the drones. This drone was originally F-80B-1-LO, S/N 45-8519. (NMUSAF)

After being retired from active and Guard units, some Shooting Stars were converted to DF-80A drone directors and QF-80 drones under Project Bad Boy. The conversions were done by the Sperry Corporation. At least one F-80B, S/N 45-8599, was converted to a drone and flown through clouds from nuclear test explosions. It was fitted with special pods under its wing tips to sample radioactive particles in the cloud. But most drones were used as targets for aerial missiles launched from other aircraft and ground-based surface-to-air missiles. The QF-80 drones could be controlled by a DF-80A drone di-rector aircraft or from the ground from a specially equipped trailer. The control equipment was installed in the nose section

in place of the machine guns and ammunition boxes. Drones could also be flown in a conventional manner by a pilot.

As was the case with other drones and drone directors, these Shooting Stars were typically painted in high visibility International Orange, but the application varied. Many were painted in an overall scheme of International Orange, but oth-ers had the high visibility color only on some areas of the air-craft. F-80As were converted to DF-80A drone directors, while examples of all fighter variants of the Shooting Star were used as drones by the Air Force. Later, the Navy would convert T-33 Shooting Stars to DT-33A drone directors and QT-33A drones.

This QF-80F, S/N 48-0889, was originally an F-80C. It has a white vertical tail, and the wings remain natural metal. The 0- in front of the serial number on the tail indicates that the aircraft is more than ten years old. It was photographed at Holloman Air Force Base, New Mexico, on March 21, 1963. (Menard Collection via NMUSAF)

Above: F-80B-1-LO, S/N 45-8641, was converted to a QF-80 drone with a whip antenna mounted forward on the nose section. Interestingly, the antenna panel for the AN/ARA-8A Radio Homing Device remains unpainted on the vertical tail. This was a feature that was unique to F-80Bs. Also note that the underwing pylon remains in place under the wing. (Menard Collection via NMUSAF)

Right: The electronics gear for the drones and drone directors was housed in the nose section in place of the six machine guns and ammunition boxes. Here, a civilian technician performs checks and maintenance on one of the drones at Wright Patterson Air Force Base, Ohio. Drones could be controlled by a DF-80 drone controller aircraft or from the ground in a trailer like the one seen in the background of this photo. (Bell Collection)

THE SHOOTING STAR IN THE KOREAN WAR

Although jet fighters became operational in relatively limited numbers with the Luftwaffe and the Royal Air Force during World War II, and two YP-80A Shooting Stars had very briefly flown visual reconnaissance missions in Italy in 1945, the Korean War was the first conflict that saw extensive use of jet fighters. The U. S. Air Force, Navy, and Marines all operated considerable numbers of jet fighters of different types in Korea along with their photographic counterparts. Two F-80C Shooting Stars of the 80th Fighter Bomber Squadron of the 8th Fighter Bomber Group are in the foreground of this photo, while Navy F9F Panthers are visible in the background. At the far end of the line of Panthers is a Marine F3D Skyknight night fighter. (NMUSAF)

The Korean War began on June 25, 1950, when troops of the North Korean People's Army (NKPA) invaded South Korea to assert North Korea's claim to be the sole legitimate government of the entire Korean peninsula. At that time, the Far East Air Force (FEAF) comprised the U. S. Air Force presence in the Western Pacific. The FEAF included the Fifth Air Force with headquarters in Japan, the Thirteenth Air Force based in the Philippines, and the Twentieth Air Force with units on Guam and Okinawa. Most of the fighter units assigned to the FEAF were equipped with F-80C Shooting Stars, although there were several squadrons of propeller-driven F-82 Twin Mustangs that performed the mission of all-weather air defense. Additionally, one F-51 Mustang squadron from the Royal Australian Air Force was attached to the Fifth Air Force.

By June 1950, most of the U. S. Navy's carrier-based fighter squadrons had converted to F9F Panthers and F2H Banshees, and Marine fighter squadrons were also operating these two types of jet fighters when the hostilities began. Accordingly, the Air Force's Shooting Stars and the Navy's and Marines' Panthers and Banshees meant that the American fighters initially committed to the United Nations forces were predominately jet types. As the war continued, additional types of jet fighters were added to the effort, including the F-94 Starfire to replace the F-82 Twin Mustang and, most notably, the F-86 Sabre by the U. S. Air Force. The Marines also added the F3D Skyknight to the conflict as an all-weather night fighter. After the Soviets and Chinese intervened, the MiG-15 Fagot was a major jet fighter participant in the war. With this

ever-increasing influx of jet fighters, the Korean War became the first war in history where jet fighters were used extensively and in far greater numbers than propeller-driven fighters.

Initially, the response by the U. S. Air Force's F-80C units was made by the Fifth Air Force. A breakdown of these units was as follows, all of which were based in Japan:

- 8th Fighter Bomber Group with the 35th FBS, 36th FBS, and 80th FBS based at Itazuke AB
- 35th Fighter Interceptor Group with the 39th FIS, 40th FIS, and 41st FIS based at Yokota AB
- 49th Fighter Bomber Group with the 7th FBS at Misawa AB, the 8th FBS at Ashiya AB, and the 9th FBS at Itazuke AB.

It should be noted that the 18th Fighter Bomber Group, assigned to the Twentieth Air Force in the Philippines, did not see any action in Korea with their F-80Cs; however, two of its squadrons converted to F-51D Mustangs and did see combat, while the third squadron remained at Clark AB to provide defense. Further, while the F-80C squadrons of the 51st Fighter Interceptor Group, assigned to the Twentieth Air Force and based on Okinawa, did not immediately see combat in Korea, two of the group's squadrons would soon join the Shooting Stars of the Fifth Air Force flying missions against the communists.

We will look at the participation of the each of the various Shooting Star units separately.

8th FIGHTER BOMBER GROUP

Three squadrons of the 80th Fighter Bomber Group initially flew missions over Korea from Japan. These included the 35th, 36th, and 80th Fighter Bomber Squadrons. For the first few weeks of the war, unit markings included wide bands near the top of their vertical tails to indicate which squadron the aircraft was assigned to. The blue band on F-80C-10-LO, S/N 49-705, indicates the 35th FBS. The squadron's blue color is also applied to the nose. "RAMBLIN=RECK=TEW" was flown by 1Lt. Robert Dewald when he shot down an Il-10 on June 27, 1950. Note the kill marking in the form of a red star on a yellow disc just below the cockpit. The Shooting Star is equipped with the elongated Misawa fuel tanks on the wing tips that significantly increased the range of the F-80C. (G. Balzer Collection)

When the North Korean invasion began, the 8th Fighter Bomber Group was based at Itazuke Air Base, Japan. At that time, its squadrons were marked with a wide band on the vertical tail in the squadron's color, these being blue for the 35th FBS, red for the 36th FBS, and yellow for the 80th FBS. Shooting Stars of these units were the first to fly into combat over Korea, seeing immediate action as the North Koreans moved south.

So fast was the advance of the North Korean People's Army that air bases in Korea were overrun, and missions had to be flown from Japan. The first missions flown by the 8th FBG were to strafe NKPA units as they moved south.

On June 26, the day after the North Koreans invaded, the 8th FBG flew missions to cover the withdrawal of American citizens, as well as some high-ranking South Koreans, and protect the evacuation efforts from attacks by the North Korean Peoples Air Force (NKPAF). Evacuations took place by ship from Inchon harbor. The following day, more evacuations took place by transport aircraft from Kimpo Air Base, and again the 8th FBG flew top cover. These sorties were flown by the 35th FBS. Because there was a considerable amount of cloud cover, F-82 Twin Mustang all-weather interceptors also covered

the evacuations. The F-82s would score the first aerial victories by USAF aircraft during the war when they shot down three Soviet-built aircraft. Very shortly thereafter, four F-80Cs of the 35th FBS engaged a group of Il-10s that were heading towards Kimpo to attack the C-54 transports that were conducting the evacuations. Four of the Il-10s were shot down, becoming the first aerial victories ever scored by an American jet aircraft. Two of the kills were scored by 1Lt. Robert Wayne and one each by Captain Ray Schillereff and 1Lt. Robert Dewald. 1Lt. Dewald was flying F-80C, S/N 49-705, that was named "RAMBLIN'=WRECK=TEW."

On June 30, the 8th FBG added to its tally of aerial victories when Lieutenants John Thomas and his wingman, Charles Wurster, each shot down a Yak-9. On July 19, Wurster would be credited with a second Yak-9, and he would be joined by Lieutenants Robert McKee and Elwood Kees, who each shot down a Yak-9. These three pilots were assigned to the 36th FBS. The following day, Lieutenants Robert Lee and David Goodenough of the 35th FBS added two more Yak-9s to the 8th FBG's score of aerial kills.

The fact that early missions had to be flown from Japan dramatized the F-80C's major shortcoming. It had very limit-

The yellow tail band on "SLICK'S CHICK" indicates assignment to the 80th FBS. This F-80C has one of the original 165-gallon tanks on the wing tips, and the squadron color is painted on the front of the tanks. The yellow squadron color is also applied to the nose, and there is a yellow band around the forward fuselage. (G. Balzer Collection)

Shortly after the war began, the 8th Fighter Bomber Group changed its markings to three flashes on the vertical tail. Blue continued to be used by the 35th Fighter Bomber Squadron, red was the color for the 36th FBS, and the 80th FBS used yellow. The group commander's aircraft had one flash of each color, and is pictured here at Suwon AB (K-13). (Escalle Collection)

Left: Loaded with two 1,000-pound bombs, an F-80C assigned to the 35th Fighter Bomber Squadron taxis across the pierced steel planking (PCP) as it heads for the active runway prior to a mission against communist targets. (NMUSAF)

Below: Ground personnel reload the ammunition boxes on an F-80C assigned to the 36th Fighter Bomber Squadron. Much of the parking areas and taxiways on Korean bases were covered with pierced steel planking. (G. Balzer Collection)

Parked on PCP and surrounded by revetments made of sand bags and 55-gallon drums, an F-80C of the 80th Fighter Bomber Squadron is loaded with 500-pound bombs as it awaits its next mission. (G. Balzer Collection)

ed range, and a mission to the area of Seoul and Inchon required a round trip more than 300 miles. Time over the target and loiter times were minimal and the Shooting Stars were armed with only their six .50-caliber machine guns. No bombs or rockets could be loaded. To correct this problem, General Earle Partridge, the commander of the Fifth Air Force, authorized the modification of the external fuel tanks carried by the Shooting Stars. The standard Fletcher tanks, which had replaced the original 165-gallon tanks on F-80s, had a single cylindrical center section. By adding two additional sections, the fuel capacity of each tank could be increased by 110 gallons, and this significantly improved the range and loiter times of the aircraft. This modification had been used unofficially the previous year, but it had never been approved, due to the additional stress on the wings during maneuvers with the much heavier tanks. But increasing the range and mission times was more important, and pilots had to be aware of limitations on maneuvers and G-forces when the tanks had a lot of fuel in them. These tanks became known as Misawa tanks, because they made effective missions possible from bases in Japan. More information about these and the other external fuel tanks can be found in the Pylons & External Stores section of the Shooting Star Details chapter.

Another action that was taken due to the F-80Cs limited range was for some units to change briefly to F-51D Mustangs. Within the 8th FBG, the 35th and 36th Fighter Bomber squadrons flew Mustangs from mid-August 1950 until they converted back to F-80Cs in December.

While other encounters with aircraft of the NKPAF took place during the early months of the war, the Allied focus was on slowing the progress of enemy ground forces. The F-80Cs, as well as other Allied aircraft, flew most of their missions attacking North Korean troops and convoys as they continued their march southward, pushing the United Nation forces down

A 1,000-pound bomb is loaded under the right wing of an F-80C of the 80th FBS. Another bomb has already been loaded under the left wing. Many of the bombs used during the Korean War were left over from World War II stockpiles, and they looked very worn and weathered. (G. Balzer Collection)

to the Pusan Perimeter where they struggled to maintain a foothold against the communist onslaught. Then on September 15, Operation Chronicle began as forces under General Douglas MacArthur launched the invasion at Inchon on the west coast of Korea to outflank and cut off the communist forces to the south. As a result, the North Koreans began a hasty and disorganized retreat to the north.

As the UN forces moved inland from Inchon, Seoul was quickly recaptured along with nearby Kimpo Air Base. In October, F-80Cs of the 80th Fighter Bomber Squadron of the 8th Fighter Bomber Group were flying missions from Kimpo while attached to the 51st Fighter Interceptor Group. As the North Koreans retreated, and the UN forces gained control of more air bases, additional USAF aircraft, including F-80Cs, began operating from them. This allowed the Shooting Stars to carry more ordnance and also spend longer times on station than was possible during missions that had been flown from Japan. F-80Cs literally flew tens of thousands of missions attacking North Korean and Chinese troops on the ground and providing close air support (CAS) to UN forces.

Not long after the war began, the 8th Fighter Bomber Group changed the markings it was using on its Shooting Stars. While the 35th, 36th, and 80th Fighter Bomber Squadrons continued to use blue, red, and yellow, respectively, as their squadron colors, the wide bands on the tails were replaced with three flashes. On some aircraft, but by no means all, these flashes were outlined in black. These markings would remain on the 8th FBG's F-80Cs for the remainder of the time the unit was equipped with Shooting Stars.

On November 25, the Chinese Army poured into Korea in large waves from the north, attacking UN forces and reinforcing the North Koreans. This initially swung the pendulum of momentum back in favor of the communists who retook Kimpo Air Base, and the Americans had to evacuate the base in January 1951. Intense fighting continued throughout the rest of 1951 with some ground gained and lost by both sides, although most of that year would be considered a stalemate. For the most part, communist forces controlled the territory north of the 38th parallel, while the UN forces maintained control south of that line.

By January 1952, the 8th Fighter Bomber Group had moved all three of its F-80C squadrons to Suwon Air Base on the west coast of Korea, and it would continue to operate from Suwon AB with its Shooting Stars until it began its transition to F-86 Sabres in 1953, shortly before the armistice was signed.

The 8th Fighter Bomber Group would operate F-80Cs longer than any other unit during the Korean war. On October 28, 1952, it flew its 50,000th sortie against the communists. While the mission included thirty-six Shooting Stars, S/N 49-591 was flown by 2Lt. Warren Guibor of the 80th FBS. This aircraft, named "The Spirit of HOBO," carried special markings on the nose to celebrate the 50,000th combat sortie flown by the group, and it was greeted by many of the unit's personnel upon its return to Suwon. By war's end, the number of sorties flown by the 8th FBG surpassed the 63,000 mark.

Among those tens of thousands of sorties, the one flown by Major Charles Loring of the 80th FBS on November 22, 1952, near Kunwha is worthy of special note. While attacking artillery batteries that were firing on UN forces, Major Loring's F-80C was severely damaged by anti-aircraft fire. Fighting the controls of his stricken aircraft, and knowing he could not make it back to base, Major Loring deliberately crashed his Shooting Star into one of the guns, causing a huge explosion, but killing him in the process. For his action, Major Loring posthumously received the Medal of Honor, and Loring AFB, Maine, was named for him.

The 80th FBS was a record-setter during the war. In March 1952, they had flown 96 sorties in a single day. But a Marine unit had broken that record in April 1953 by flying 117 sorties. Two weeks later, the 80th FBS, by then the only remaining Shooting Star squadron in Korea with twenty F-80Cs, regained the record by flying 120 sorties on April 24 without a single abort and without any losses. Approximately two weeks later, on May 6, the 80th FBS flew its final combat missions in the F-80C, and these would be the last time a fighter version of the Shooting Star would fly in combat with the USAF. The squadron then began its transition to the F-86F Sabre.

2Lt. Warren Guibor taxis to the parking area at Suwon after completing the 50,000th combat sortie flown by the 8th Fighter Bomber Group in Korea. The 8th FBG flew F-80s longer than any other unit in the war. This photo is dated October 28, 1952. The aircraft was named "The Spirit of HOBO," and it had a cartoon hobo character painted on the nose, along with a banner proclaiming the 50,000th mission. (G. Balzer Collection)

The 49th Fighter Bomber Group was the second unit equipped with F-80Cs to fly combat missions in Korea, joining the 8th FBG during the first days of the war. The 49th FBG included the 7th, 8th, and 9th Fighter Bomber Squadrons. Initially flying missions from bases in Japan, later in the war the 49th FBG operated out of Taegu Air Base in Korea. Here, F-80Cs from the 49th FBS head home following a mission against communist targets. Note the Misawa tanks on the wing tips. (NMUSAF)

The 49th Fighter Bomber Group, consisting of the 7th, 8th, and 9th Fighter Bomber Squadrons, was the second F-80C group to fly combat missions during the war, joining the 8th FBG only a day later on June 27, 1950. Normally based at Misawa AB, the unit was away participating in an exercise when the North Koreans invaded. It was immediately ordered to Itazuke AB to join with the 8th FBG and begin combat operations. Its first squadron to see action was the 9th FBS which flew its first sorties on June 27. Two days later, it achieved its first aerial victory when 1Lt. William Norris shot down an LA-7 while covering the evacuation of U. S. personnel at Kimpo AB.

In late September, after the successful landings at Inchon, the 49th FBG moved from Japan to Taegu Air Base (K-2), near the southern tip of South Korea, and within the Pusan Perimeter, where it continued operations with its Shooting Stars for a few months until June 1951. That month, the group transitioned to the F-84 Thunderjet. As this transition took place, the group's F-80Cs were transferred to other F-80C units to replace aircraft losses. This marked the introduction of the F-84 into the conflict, and from this point in time, the number of F-84Es and F-84Gs continued to increase, while the number of F-80Cs decreased.

The 49th Fighter Group insignia is just visible on the open gun bay door of this F-80C as it undergoes an engine change at Taegu Air Base in 1951. The blue marking on the nose indicates assignment to the 7th Fighter Bomber Squadron. Another airman stands on one of the ammunition boxes as he checks out the radio gear at the aft end of the nose compartment. (Bell Collection)

51ˢᵗ FIGHTER INTERCEPTOR GROUP

Colonel Irwin H. Dregne, CO of the 51ˢᵗ Fighter Interceptor Group, flew F-80C-10-LO, S/N 49-665. He named his Shooting Star "The Dregs," and it displayed a considerable number of red mission markings on the side of the fuselage. 5-inch rockets were loaded under the wings when this photograph was taken. The blue color on the nose represented the 16ᵗʰ FIS, while the red stripes on the vertical tail were for the 25ᵗʰ FIS. These were the two squadrons from the 51ˢᵗ FIG that flew combat missions during the Korean War. (Menard Collection via the NMUSAF)

To increase the number of F-80 units in Korea, the 51ˢᵗ FIG on Okinawa was ordered to send two of its squadrons, the 16ᵗʰ FIS and the 25ᵗʰ FIS, to Itazuke Air Base, Japan, while the 26ᵗʰ FIS remained on Okinawa to provide air defense. By October 10, these two squadrons moved to Kimpo (K-14), along with the 80ᵗʰ FBS of the 8ᵗʰ FBG which was attached to the 51ˢᵗ FIG

for this move. (The 8ᵗʰ Fighter Bomber Group's 35ᵗʰ FBS and 36ᵗʰ FBS were temporarily flying F-51D Mustangs at that time.) For the next two and a half months, these three squadrons flew combat missions from Kimpo until January 1951 when the base was retaken by the communists, and the USAF units there had to evacuate.

A Shooting Star assigned to the 25ᵗʰ Fighter Interceptor Squadron of the 51ˢᵗ Fighter Interceptor Group is about ready to take the active runway for a mission from Kimpo Air Base (K-14). Red was the squadron color for the 25ᵗʰ FIS. The Shooting Star is fitted with standard Fletcher external tanks. (Menard Collection via NMUSAF)

This profile illustrates the F-80C-10-LO, S/N 49-713, flown by 1Lt. Russell J. Brown of the 16ᵗʰ Fighter Interceptor Squadron of the 51ˢᵗ Fighter Interceptor Group on November 8, 1950, when he shot down a MiG-15. This is believed to be the first jet-on-jet aerial victory in history. Note the kill marking on the fuselage just beneath the canopy rail. The 51ˢᵗ FIG used a large flash on the nose and one or two stripes on the vertical tail as its markings. The blue color signified the 16ᵗʰ FIS. (Roszak)

The first MiG-15s appeared over Korea in early November 1950, during the time the 51st FIG was flying out of Kimpo. This was a complete surprise to the UN forces, as intelligence efforts had not previously revealed the existence of the Soviet-built fighter. The swept-wing fighter was clearly superior to the F-80C in both speed and maneuverability, and it posed a major threat to all UN aircraft in the war. However, it was the F-80 that would score the first jet-on-jet aerial victory when 1Lt. Russell Brown, a pilot in the 16th FIS, shot down a MiG-15 on November 8, 1950.

After retreating back to Japan when Kimpo was retaken by the communists in January 1951, the two squadrons of the 51st FIG continued operations from there until moving to Taegu AB (K-2), where they would fly missions with their Shooting Stars for several more months until November 1951. Being a fighter interceptor group, and primarily trained in air-to-air combat, the unit then transitioned to the F-86E Sabre as more Sabres were introduced into the conflict to counter the MiG-15s. Again, most of its F-80s were reassigned to remaining units that were still flying the Shooting Star.

35th FIGHTER INTERCEPTOR GROUP

When the North Koreans invaded South Korea on June 25, 1950, the 35th Fighter Interceptor Group was equipped with F-80Cs and based at Ashiya Air Base, Japan. Its squadrons, the 39th, 40th, and 41st Fighter Interceptor Squadrons, were equipped with F-80Cs. However, the 40th FIS transitioned to F-51D Mustangs within a few months. Some sources state that the 39th FIS also operated F-51Ds in Korea. This was part of the attempt to get more fighter-bombers into action with a longer range and mission endurance capability than the F-80C.

The 35th FIG moved around a lot during 1950 and into early 1951. In July, the group moved to Pohang Air Base (K-3); however, the advancing North Korean forces necessitated a move back to Tsuiki Air Base, Japan, the following month. In December, the unit moved to Pusan AB on the southern tip of the Korean peninsula. It then moved to Suwon AB in March 1951, but the following month it moved again to the Yeouido AB (K-16) near Seoul.

In May 1951, the 35th FIG was moved back to Johnson Air Base, Japan, where it was re-equipped and assigned the mission of providing air defense for Japan.

SUMMARY

When the last mission by F-80Cs was flown in Korea on May, 6, 1953, the Shooting Stars had scored seventeen aerial victories and destroyed at least twenty-four enemy aircraft on the ground. But their contribution to the war effort was immensely more important in the fighter-bomber role. They flew countless missions attacking communist forces and convoys on the ground while supporting the UN forces with close air support missions. They attacked and destroyed bridges, trains, artillery emplacements, supply dumps and storage areas, and cratered runways on airfields. Once they could operate from bases within South Korea, they proved to be very effective in the fighter-bomber role while maintaining a high state of operational readiness. But the success was not without losses. A total of 277 Shooting Stars were lost in combat; 133 to ground fire, 14 to enemy aircraft, and the rest to unknown causes. Additionally, 96 were operational losses not due to combat.

The yellow lightning bolt on the fuselage and the yellow band on the tail of this F-80C indicate that it was assigned to the 41st Fighter Interceptor Squadron of the 35th Fighter Interceptor Group. This photograph was taken at Pohang Air Base (K-3), Korea. Soon after the war began, the 35th FIG transitioned to the F-51D Mustang which it would fly in combat until May 1951. (NMUSAF)

RECON SHOOTING STARS IN KOREA

Left & Above: RF-80A, S/N 44-85467, which was assigned to the 45th Tactical Reconnaissance Squadron of the 67th Tactical Reconnaissance Wing, was unusual in that it had Olive Drab painted on its upper and vertical surfaces. Almost all RF-80s that took part in the Korean War were in a natural metal scheme. The photo at left provides a good look at some of the flight gear worn by fighter pilots in Korea. (Both, NMUSAF)

RF-80As played a significant role during the Korean War. Their value in gathering photographic intelligence was so great that the USAF gave them top priority for maintenance and parts to keep them operational at the highest possible levels. When the war began, twenty-five RF-80As were assigned to the 8th Tactical Reconnaissance Squadron based at Yokota AB in Japan under operational control of the 35th Fighter Bomber Group.

Two days after the North Koreans invaded, the 8th TRS moved four RF-80As to Itazuke to position them closer to South Korea. The first missions by the squadron were flown the following day to assess the situation in and around Seoul, where the evacuation of American citizens was underway.

This was to determine how close the units of the NKPA were to that area. The tactical reconnaissance assets would soon be increased with the addition of Marine F4U-5P Corsairs, F7F-3P Tigercats, F2H-2P Banshees, and Navy F9F-2P Panthers. The Air Force would add RF-86 Sabres, RB-26 Invaders, and RF-51D Mustangs. But during the critical early weeks of the war, as the NKPA pushed southward, this important mission fell almost entirely on the RF-80As of the 8th TRS. They provided valuable intelligence of enemy troop movements, and prior to Operation Chromite, they took vital photos of the tides at Inchon which were among the most extreme anywhere in the world.

As more reconnaissance assets were added to the war effort by the FEAF, the 67th Tactical Reconnaissance Wing was

The RF-80As of the 8th TRS received the highest priority for maintenance and spare parts to keep them mission-ready during the early months of the war when the burden for tactical reconnaissance within the USAF fell primarily on the squadron. Here, maintenance, including an engine change is being performed on the unit's RF-80As at Hazuke Air Base, Japan, shortly after the war began. (NMUSAF)

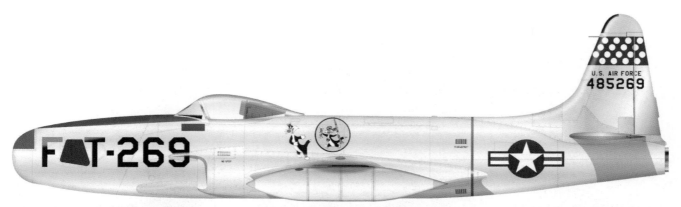

RF-80A, S/N 44-85269, has the blue band with the white polka dots that indicate assignment to the 45th TRS. However, it is in the usual natural metal finish found on almost all Shooting Stars in Korea. (Roszak)

The white tail band on "Darlin Doris" indicates that RF-80A, S/N 45-8373, was assigned to the 15th Tactical Reconnaissance Squadron. Missions flown were indicated in the form of red camera markings on the forward fuselage. (Roszak)

activated in late February 1951. The 8th TRS was assigned to the wing, but it was redesignated the 15th TRS. Other units included the 45th TRS, initially equipped with RF-51 Mustangs, and the 12th TRS with RB-26 Invaders for night reconnaissance. The 67th TRW began its operations out of Taegu AB, South Korea. It would remain at Taegu until August 1951, when it moved to Kimpo AB, where it would remain for the rest of the war. By the end of 1951, the 45th TRS had begun replacing its RF-51s with RF-80As, giving the 67th TRW two RF-80A squadrons.

There always seemed to be a shortage of RF-80As, and crews worked tirelessly to keep them operational. To increase the numbers, even a small amount, several F-80Cs were modified to RF-80Cs. These retained two of the .50-caliber machine guns while still having mounts for several cameras. They also had the advantage of having ejection seats which the RF-80As did not. Other F-80Cs had full camera noses installed to replace their gun noses.

The RF-80s continued to fly photo-reconnaissance missions throughout the rest of the war, providing valuable information about enemy troop movements and other activities. They also flew pre- and post-strike sorties to determine the effectiveness of attacks on targets. But after the MiG-15 entered combat, the slower RF-80s were easy prey for the much faster MiGs, so they had to be escorted by F-86 Sabres when they flew in the areas were the MiG-15s operated. Late in the war, several F-86As and F-86Es, modified with camera installations and redesignated as RF-86s, were added to the inventory of

the 15th TRS, and still later, production RF-86Fs were acquired during the final few months of the war. But even with these additions, the RF-80s remained active until July 27, 1953, when the conflict finally came to an end.

The 15th TRS also had yellow tail bands on some of its RF-80As. Here, pilots and ground crew personnel discuss operations as one of their photo recon Shooting Stars, named "MMA-DEE," is serviced and checked. Note the different styles and colors of flight suits on the pilots. (Escalle Collection)

SHOOTING STAR DETAILS
COCKPIT DETAILS
XP-80 PROTOTYPE COCKPIT DETAILS

1. AMMETER
2. COMPASS CORRECTION CARD HOLDER
3. REMOTE INDICATING COMPASS
4. CLOCK
5. GYRO HORIZON
6. DIRECTIONAL GYRO
7. ENGINE TACHOMETER
8. JET TEMPERATURE
9. SUCTION GAGE
10. SUCTION GAGE SELECTOR SWITCH
11. BURNER RING FUEL PRESSURE
12. REAR BEARING TEMPERATURE
13. RATE OF CLIMB INDICATOR LOCATION (TEST INSTRUMENT SHOWN)
14. TURN AND BANK INDICATOR
15. AIRSPEED INDICATOR
16. ALTIMETER
17. FUEL BOOST PRESSURE WARNING LIGHT
18. FUEL LOW LEVEL WARNING LIGHT
19. FUSELAGE TANK FUEL QUANTITY GAGE
20. LANDING GEAR POSITION INDICATOR LIGHTS
21. HYDRAULIC PRESSURE GAGE
22. LANDING GEAR DOWN WARNING LIGHTS
23. ACCELEROMETER (TEST INSTRUMENT)
24. OXYGEN FLOW INDICATOR
25. OXYGEN PRESSURE GAGE
26. OIL PRESSURE GAGE
27. ELEVATOR TAB CONTROL SWITCH
28. BUTTON NOT USED- MACHINE GUN TRIGGER FORWARD SIDE
29. REAR ENGINE BEARING OIL FLOW WARNING LIGHT
30. REAR ENGINE BEARING OIL PRESSURE WARNING LIGHT
31. PARKING BRAKE LEVER
32. OXYGEN LOW PRESSURE WARNING LIGHT

The instruments and other details of the cockpit in the XP-80 prototype are illustrated and identified in these three photographs that were used in the manual for the aircraft. (All, NMUSAF)

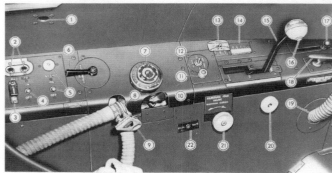

1. COCKPIT VENTILATING AIR EXIT
2. SCR-695 RADIO DESTRUCTOR BUTTONS
3. SCR-695 RADIO EMERGENCY SWITCH
4. SCR-695 RADIO OFF-ON SWITCH
5. SCR-695 RADIO "G" BAND SWITCHES
6. AILERON CONTROL BOOST SHUTOFF VALVE
7. OXYGEN REGULATOR ALTITUDE VALVE
8. OXYGEN MASK CONNECTION
9. OXYGEN SUPPLY TUBE CLOTHES CLIP
10. DILUTER LEVER
11. ELEVATOR TAB POSITION INDICATOR LIGHT
12. ELEVATOR TAB CONTROL SWITCH
13. WING FLAP CONTROL SWITCH
14. WING FLAP POSITION INDICATOR
15. THROTTLE LEVER
16. RADIO MICROPHONE BUTTON
17. COCKPIT HEAT CONTROL
18. FIRE EXTINGUISHER CONTROL (TEST EQUIPMENT)
19. WINDSHIELD DEFROSTER TUBE (STOWED)
20. THROTTLE FRICTION CONTROL
21. ALTITUDE IDLE VALVE
22. ELEVATOR TAB CIRCUIT BREAKER RESET BUTTON

1. COCKPIT VENTILATOR
2. BATTERY SWITCH
3. GENERATOR SWITCH
4. FUEL TRANSFER PUMP ON INDICATOR LIGHTS
5. FUEL TRANSFER PUMP SWITCH
6. FUEL BOOST PUMP CIRCUIT BREAKER RESET
7. FUEL BOOST PUMP SWITCH
8. STARTER SAFETY SWITCH
9. STARTER SAFETY CIRCUIT BREAKER RESET
10. STARTER SWITCH
11. IGNITER PLUGS SWITCH
12. IGNITER PLUGS CIRCUIT BREAKER RESET
13. EMISSION SELECTOR SWITCH
14. TRANSMITTER KEY
15. TRANSMITTER SELECTOR SWITCH
16. HEADSET SELECTOR SWITCHES
17. MAIN POWER SWITCH (RECEIVERS)
18. RADIO RANGE FILTER SWITCH
19. TEL. PLUG (IN "B" JACK)
20. TUNING CRANKS
21. VOLUME CONTROLS
22. MAIN POWER SWITCH (TRANSMITTERS)
23. GUNSIGHT LIGHT RHEOSTAT
24. ARMAMENT MASTER SWITCH
25. ARMAMENT HEATER SWITCH
26. ARMAMENT CIRCUIT BREAKER RESET
27. PITOT HEATER SWITCH
28. LANDING GEAR WARNING HORN SWITCH
29. COCKPIT HEATER OUTLET
30. GUNSIGHT CIRCUIT BREAKER RESET
31. 274N RADIO CIRCUIT BREAKER RESET
32. FUEL QUANTITY GAGE CIRCUIT BREAKER
33. PRESSURE LIGHTS CIRCUIT BREAKER RESET
34. COMPASS CIRCUIT BREAKER RESET
35. LANDING GEAR CIRCUIT BREAKER RESET
36. HYDRAULIC HAND PUMP
37. LANDING GEAR EMERGENCY EXTENTION SOURCE SELECTOR VALVE
38. MICROPHONE AND HEADSET JACK CORDS

P-80A COCKPIT DETAILS

Above: The details in the cockpit directly beneath the windscreen in a P-80A are revealed in this photograph. The dominant feature is the K-14 gunsight with its reflecting glass on top. The two small instruments that are visible low and to the left on the instrument panel are the oxygen flow gage (Blinker) and the oxygen pressure gage. (NMUSAF)

Right: The instrument panel in the P-80A was not all that different from those in propeller-driven fighters of the late 1940s. Flying and navigation instruments were on the upper main part of the panel along with the fuel pressure gage and the tail pipe temperature gage. Other engine and system related instruments were on the lower section of the panel. Also note the various check lists. The one at top left indicates that this aircraft is an early P-80-1-LO. (NMUSAF)

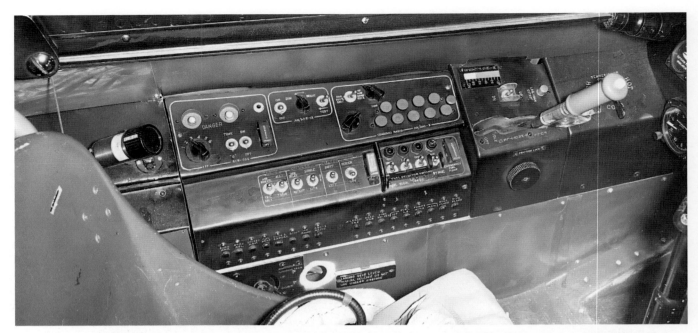

Details on the left side of the cockpit in an early P-80A are illustrated in this photograph. This was quite different than that in the prototype and the early developmental Shooting Stars, but the items on this console and their arrangement would change during P-80A production. The cabin temperature control was at the forward end of the console with the throttle directly aft of it. The friction control knob for the throttle was located beneath it on the vertical side of the console. The flap controls were inboard of the throttle. Fuel selector switches were aft of the throttle, and inboard of those switches was the panel that controlled the AN/ARC-3 Command Radio. The AN/APS-13 control panel was aft of that, and inboard of it were the armament control switches. The IFF and SCR-695 control panel was farther aft. Circuit breakers and the landing gear controls were on the vertical side beneath the console. (NMUSAF)

Numerous switches were on the right console in the cockpit in early P-80As. At the forward end of the console was a line of switches. From front to rear, these were the ignition booster switch, the starter switch, the battery master switch, the generator switch, the hydraulic pump motor switch, the pitot heat switch, and the landing light switch. Aft of these switches was a panel that controlled the identification lights. On the vertical panel beneath all of these switches was a panel of circuit breakers. Aft of the switches on the console was a circular panel with a socket and controls for the headphones. On later P-80As and subsequent variants, the identification lights were deleted, and this area contained the VHF radio controls. Farther aft is the gage that indicates cabin pressure, and above and slightly behind it is the fluorescent cabin light. Note the data information that states that this is a P-80A-1-LO. The fixed seat used in the P-80A is also partly visible in this photograph and the one above. A map case was located to the right of the seat. (NMUSAF)

F-80C COCKPIT DETAILS

All: The cockpit in the F-80C was generally the same as the F-80A and F-80B that came before it, with only detail changes in the arrangement of the instruments and other items. Shooting Star cockpits were usually painted flat black with a Dark Gull Gray cockpit floor. These three photographs provide a good look at the instrument panel with the flying and navigation instruments on the main upper panel and engine and system instruments below them. The exhaust temperature gage and the engine RPM gage are low and to the right on the upper part of the panel. The K-14 gunsight remained at the top of the panel, while checklists remain near the center. The grip at the top of the control column is also visible. (All, Kinzey)

The same items found on the left console in the previous variants were also in the F-80C. These included the cockpit temperature control at the forward end and the throttle aft of it. Between them was the landing gear warning horn shutoff switch. Switches to jettison bombs and external fuel tanks were above the forward panel. Moving aft, the upper panel with the red covers on the switches and dials was the AN/ARC-3 control panel. The panel inboard of that controlled the fuel system. Aft of that panel was the armament control panel for the bombs and rockets. In this aircraft, switches to jettison external stores are on the upper part of the console at the aft end, but some F-80Cs had a panel for the SCR-695 radio in this location. The connection for the oxygen hose is visible just below the arm of the ejection seat. (Kinzey)

The switch with the red guard on the upper right side of the cockpit opened and closed the later style canopy that was operated electrically. Below it was a panel with eight switches. From left to right, these were the ignition normal-off switch, the starter switch, the battery master switch, the pitot heater switch, the landing and taxi light switch, the fuselage lights switch, the navigation lights dim-bright switch, and the navigation lights steady-flash switch. On the next step down were several circuit breakers with the inverter test switch aft of them. Additional circuit breakers were located on the vertical side of the console. Obscured behind the arm rest for the ejection seat were the cockpit temperature gage and the cockpit altimeter. Aft of those was the code selector and signal light switch. (Kinzey)

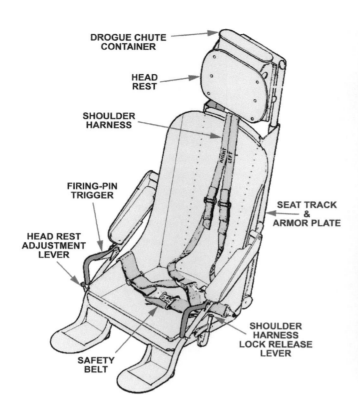

DROGUE CHUTE
CONTAINER

HEAD
REST

SHOULDER
HARNESS

FIRING-PIN
TRIGGER

HEAD REST
ADJUSTMENT
LEVER

SEAT TRACK
&
ARMOR PLATE

SHOULDER
HARNESS
LOCK RELEASE
LEVER

SAFETY
BELT

The F-80B and F-80C were equipped with an early ejection seat. Power for ejection was provided by a cartridge at the back of the seat. Most seats simply had a metal head rest, but some had a pad attached to the headrest. The major components of the seat are identified in this drawing that is based on one from the pilot's manual for the F-80B and F-80C. (Roszak)

The seat in the F-80C on display at the U. S. Air Force Armament Museum has the pad installed on the headrest. While these pads were often red, vintage photos show some to be other colors including gray and an olive green. Red pads were often on the arm rests as well. This seat is painted Dark Gull Gray, but vintage photographs provide evidence that some were other colors, including a darker gray and a shade of olive green. (Kinzey)

The seat was a bucket design, and there was no parachute or survival kit packed with it. Instead, the pilot wore these two items as part of his flight gear. The survival kit fit in the bucket and served as a cushion, while the parachute was a cushion between the pilot's back and the seat. The arm rests are shown in the raised position in this photograph. (Kinzey)

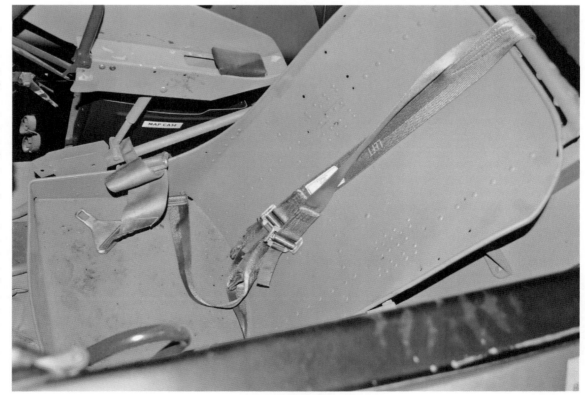

WINDSCREEN & CANOPY DETAILS

The original windscreen and canopy used on early Shooting Stars consisted of a fixed three-piece windscreen and a bubble canopy much like that used on late variants of the P-47 Thunderbolt and the P-51 Mustang. It was mechanically-operated by a hand crank inside the cockpit on the right side. An external hand crank was located under an access panel beneath the windscreen on the right side of the fuselage. Early P-80As/F-80As had a wire antenna for the command radio that ran from the leading edge of the vertical tail and entered the cockpit though the canopy as seen here. Its forward end attached to the back of the armor plate above the fixed seat in the cockpit. The original canopy had a pointed aft end on its framework. (G. Balzer Collection)

Above: The original canopy was also initially fitted to the RF-80A. The antenna wire was later deleted, and an AN/ARN-6 Radio Sense Antenna was embedded into the top of the canopy. Note the different armor plate with a very narrow headrest in this aircraft. This original canopy was also initially fitted to F-80Bs and early F-80Cs. Some windscreens on early Shooting Stars had a triangular-shaped piece of metal added at the bottom of each side of the framework as seen here. (G. Balzer Collection)

Right: Additional details of the windscreen are visible in this view. The hand crank lever and chain for the original manually-operated canopy is visible on the right side of the cockpit just below the aft part of the windscreen. (NMUSAF)

The original canopy was replaced with an electrically-operated unit that could be identified by a fairing that extended rearward from the aft end of the framework. It was retrofitted to existing Shooting Stars as evidenced on this F-80A-10-LO. For the F-80As that had the antenna wire, the replacement canopies had the opening for the wire, and the sense antenna was not present. The new canopy was also retrofitted to RF-80s. (G. Balzer Collection)

The new electrically-operated canopy was retrofitted to F-80Bs and early F-80Cs that had the original manually-operated canopy, and it became the production standard for late production F-80Cs. This canopy did have the sense antenna embedded into it. This version of the later canopy is shown here on an F-80C-10-LO. (G. Balzer Collection)

The canopy on the F-80C that is displayed at the U. S. Air Force Armament Museum is simply placed on top of the fuselage aft of the cockpit, and it is not connected to its rails inside the cockpit. This places the canopy farther aft on top of the fuselage than it would be on an operational aircraft. However, these two photographs are included to show the details of the rails aft of the seat that were part of the mechanism on which the canopy moved fore and aft as well as the structure inside the aft end of the canopy. The small yellow item seen in the photo at left is the manual canopy release. (Both, Kinzey)

FUSELAGE DETAILS

On the two XP-80As, the thirteen YP-80As, and early production P-80As, a landing/taxi light was located under a conformal lens at the top of the nose above the machine guns. (G. Balzer Collection)

On each side of the fuselage, just above and below the engine inlet, was a series of vents. These ducted boundary layer air between the fuselage and the inlet ramp out of the aircraft. On F-80B and F-80C variants, two small panels were located beneath the windscreen on the right side. The smaller top panel provided access to the switch that opened and closed the later electrically-operated canopy. On early F-80s and RF-80s with the manually-operated canopy, an external hand crank to operate the canopy was in approximately this same position. The lower panel covered the emergency canopy jettison switch. The panel aft of the warning stencil covers the filler point for the emergency hydraulic tank. Note also the fueling point for the fuselage tank next to the aft end of the canopy that is indicated by the red outline. A grounding point is aft of it, indicated by the black disc marking. (Flegal)

During P-80A production, the landing/taxi lights were moved to a position at the top of the nose gear strut. A black radome that covered the AN/ARN-6 Compass Loop Antenna replaced the lights on the nose above the machine guns. This would remain standard for all subsequent F-80 production aircraft. The black radome and the relocated landing/taxi lights are both visible in this photograph. (Escalle Collection)

There was no crank or switch to operate the canopy on the left side of the fuselage. Instead, a stencil above the vents stated that the canopy was to be operated externally on the right side of the aircraft. On F-80Bs and F-80Cs, there was usually another stencil above it warning that the aircraft was fitted with canopy and ejection seat containing explosive charges. NO STEP stencils were below the vents on each side, warning personnel not to use them as steps to climb on the aircraft. (Kinzey)

Left: Entry and egress to the cockpit was made possible by a boarding ladder designed specifically for the F-80. It could be used on either side of the aircraft, and it was commonly positioned on the right side, because the external operating crank or switch for the canopy was only on that side. This departed from most USAF jet fighters where cockpit access was almost always only on the left side. Lockheed's future F-104 Starfighter was an exception. This photo shows the ladder on the right side of the F-80C assigned to the commander of the 49th TFG. (NMUSAF)

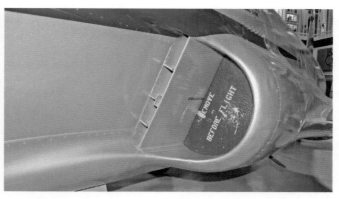

Air for the J33 engine was taken in through two semi-circular inlets, one on each side of the fuselage. The inner wall of the inlet was separated from the fuselage by a ramp. Boundary layer air that was taken in between the fuselage and the ramp was discharged from the aircraft through vents above and below the inlets. Interestingly, the gun camera was mounted inside the right inlet at the nine-o'clock position, and it is visible in the photo at left. The access to the oxygen filler valve was on the inner wall near the front of the left inlet. (Both, Kinzey)

Two large panels on top of the fuselage provided access to the forward engine compartment. Each panel had a blow-in door to provide auxiliary air to the engine when it was idling or at low taxi speeds. A clear position light was aft of these panels. The red beacon light, seen in these two photographs, was an addition to the Shooting Star very late in its operational service. It should be noted that the canopy on this F-80C, which is on display at the U. S. Air Force Armament Museum, is simply placed on the aircraft aft of the cockpit, and it is farther aft than it would be on an operational aircraft. On an operational aircraft with the canopy properly installed, the aft end would not extend back onto the two panels. (Both, Kinzey)

On some F-80Bs and all F-80Cs, small vents were added on the aft fuselage in four places to improve cooling in the engine compartment. The upper vent on the right side is visible in the photograph at left. The top vent on the left side is visible in the photograph at right, and the lower vent is just visible at the bottom of the fuselage below the wing root. Slots were on the fairings at the aft end of the wing roots. The access panel that is in the upper area of the national insignias on each side provided access to the connection between the aft end of the engine and the tail pipe. (Left, Flegal; Right, Kinzey)

A series of four vents were on the underside of the fuselage, just aft of the nose gear. The outer two vents were under the air inlets for the engine and were the same size as the vents near the top of each inlet on the sides of the fuselage. They had the same purpose as the vents above the inlet, that of venting boundary layer air between the fuselage and the inlet ramp out of the aircraft. (Kinzey)

Two small scoops were located on the underside of the fuselage, just outboard of the speed brakes near their leading edge. This is the scoop to the right of the speed brakes. (Kinzey)

The left scoop is visible in this photograph. The red fuel vent aft of it was an addition that was made late in the service life of the F-80. The speed brakes are in the closed position in this photograph. (Kinzey)

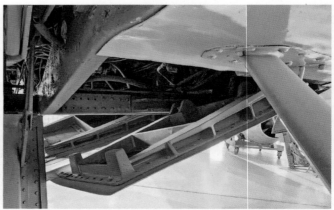

The two speed brakes are shown in the partially open position in these two photographs. The inside surface of each brake was painted red. (Both, Manning)

Above left and right: The use of JATO bottles for assisted take-off was first tested on YP-80A, S/N 44-83031. This capability was standard on all operational variants of the Shooting Star. The attachment points for the two JATO bottles under the aft fuselage are illustrated in these two photographs. Each JATO unit was attached by a single clip near the front and two more points farther aft. Note the clear light aft of the attachment points in the photo at left. (Both, Kinzey)

Right: Inert JATO bottles are mounted in place under the aft fuselage. The manual instructed pilots that the JATO units could be fired at any time during the takeoff roll, but it was best not to fire them until the aircraft was close to rotation speed. (Kinzey)

Two F-80Cs from the 51st Fighter Interceptor Group take off from a Korean base using JATO units. These were often used during the hot Korean summers when the density altitude was high; however, the F-80C required the use of JATO units far less often than the F-84 Thunderjets that began to replace them in the air war over Korea. (NMUSAF)

67

WING DETAILS

P-80s/F-80s had a straight wing with a conventional airfoil shape. The wing tips were rounded and a navigation light was on the edge of each tip. The light on the right wing tip was a blue color when not illuminated, and the one of the left wing tip was red. (Both, Manning)

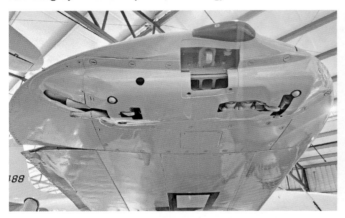

Each wing tip was a hardpoint for carrying external stores. In most cases, external fuel tanks were carried under the wing tips; however, bombs up to the 1,000-pound size could also be loaded under each tip. The attachment points under both wing tips are shown in these two photographs. (Both, Manning)

The right aileron had a fixed tab on the trailing edge at its inboard end, as illustrated in the photo at left. A movable trim tab was located at the inboard end of the left aileron as shown in the photo at right. Unlike the fixed tab on the right aileron, it was flush with the trailing edge of the aileron, rather than extending aft of it. (Both, Kinzey)

Most Shooting Stars had a non-skid black walkway on top of each wing at the root. This walkway usually extended from the leading edge back to the no-step area above the flap. In some cases, the forward end of the walkway stopped a few inches short of the leading edge. It should be noted that some vintage photographs do show Shooting Stars without these walkways, but they were usually present. (Kinzey)

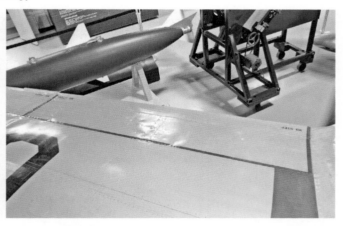

Flaps were located on the inboard section of each wing and extended from the wing root out to the aileron. Because the top of the wing above the flap was much thinner than the rest of the wing, it was outlined in red to mark it as a no-step area. (Both, Kinzey)

The left and right flaps are shown in the lowered position in these two views, revealing the details on the inner surfaces. Note that the trailing edge of the wing is actually part of the flap. On early P-80s/F-80s, the inner surfaces were often painted Chromate Green or Interior Green, but on later Shooting Stars they were painted silver or left bare metal. The three NO STEP markings above each flap, as seen in these two photographs, are in the most common arrangement for these markings as used on F-80s. (Both, Manning)

Above and right: There were two fueling points for the wing tanks on top of each wing with a grounding point near each. One of the fueling points was near the wing tip with the grounding point aft of it. The fueling points were usually outlined in red, and the grounding points were identified by a black disc marking. The photo above shows the fueling point for the outboard wing tank in the left wing, with the grounding point aft of it and nearer the tip. At right are the outboard fueling and grounding points on the right wing. (Both, Noack)

An airman refuels an RF-80A at the inboard fueling point on top of the left wing. Note the wire attached to the grounding point to prevent a static electric charge from possibly causing a spark that could ignite the fuel. The fueling and grounding points on top of the right wing were simply a mirror image of the left wing. (Bell Collection)

A pilot of the 80th Fighter Bomber Squadron of the 8th Fighter Bomber Wing poses with his F-80C in Korea. A 1,000-pound bomb is loaded under the left wing. What is noteworthy is the device on the leading edge of the wing at the extreme right side of the photograph. These were added to both wings on some, but certainly not all, Shooting Stars in Korea. In addition to the gun camera that was located inside the right inlet, these provided documentation of the delivery of ordnance against communist targets. (Escalle Collection)

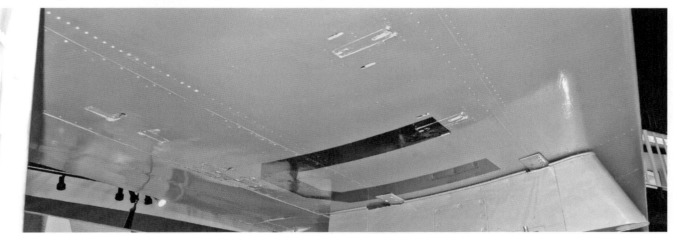

Above: The stubs for mounting 5-inch rockets were located between the pylon and the landing gear under each wing. These were retractable, and they folded up flush with the wing when not being used. The single forward stub attached to the body of the rocket, while the two smaller aft stubs attached to the two upper fins. The stubs under the left wing are illustrated in this photograph. Photos of extended stubs, with and without rockets attached, can be found in the Pylons & External Stores section of this chapter. (Kinzey)

Right: The stubs for mounting 5-inch rockets under the right wing are visible in this photo. Forward is to the left of the photo. (Kinzey)

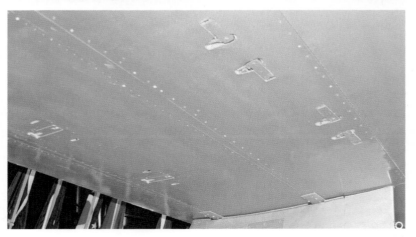

LANDING GEAR DETAILS
NOSE LANDING GEAR DETAILS

There were two types of nose gear wheels used on F-80s. The first was a heavy spoked design with triangular-shaped openings between the spokes. On this museum aircraft, the scissors link on the oleo has been disconnected, and the oleo is compressed, because there is no hydraulic pressure in the strut. (Both, Noack)

The second and more common nose gear wheel was solid, but it did have spokes on each side. Shooting Stars had a single fork design for the nose gear strut. The photo left is of an F-80C, while the one at right is of an early P-80A which had the landing/taxi light on the nose. (Left, Noack; Right, Manning)

Above and right: During late production of the P-80A, the landing/taxi light was replaced with a radome covering the AN/ARN-6 Compass Loop Antenna on the nose, and a dual landing/taxi light arrangement was mounted at the top of the nose gear strut. The closeup above provides a detailed look at the light installation on the nose gear strut. Note the later L-shaped pitot probe forward of the nose gear. At right is an overall view of the nose gear with the lights in place. (Both, Kinzey)

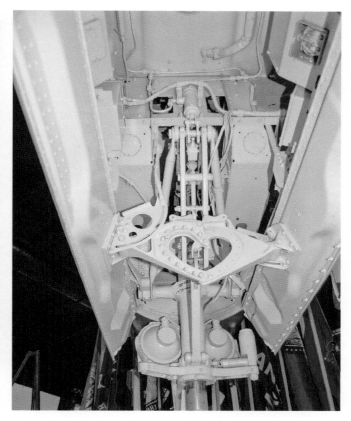

Details on the aft end of the nose gear strut, fork, wheel, and light assembly are revealed in this view. It should be noted that the wheel wells and struts on operational P-80s/F-80s were not usually painted white as they are on this museum aircraft. Most often, the struts were a steel or aluminum color, while the wheel wells were painted Interior Green or silver. (Kinzey)

This view looks up and forward into the nose gear well and shows the drag link for the strut and other details, including the actuators for the nose gear doors. The back of the landing/taxi lights are also visible. (Kinzey)

Left and above: Details inside the aft end of the nose gear well are illustrated in the photo at left. A canvas cover was usually at the aft end of the well to prevent debris from getting into the fuselage as seen in the photo at right. (Both, Kinzey)

LEFT MAIN LANDING GEAR DETAILS

Above: The left landing gear is shown from the outboard side and slightly in front in this view. The two outer doors overlapped when the gear was extended. The lower door was attached to the strut, while the upper door was hinged at the outer end of the well. (Kinzey)

Right: Details of the left landing gear are revealed here. The drag strut, the hydraulic cylinder that actuated the gear, and the scissors link are all visible. The main gear wheels usually were the solid spoked design shown here. (Kinzey)

Above and right: Additional details of the left landing gear are illustrated in these two views. The photo at left was taken from behind the gear, while the one at right was taken from in front and slightly to the inside. (Above, Kinzey; Right, Manning)

The later wheel design used on the main gear was a flat disc design with a series of holes around the edge next to the rim. (Kinzey)

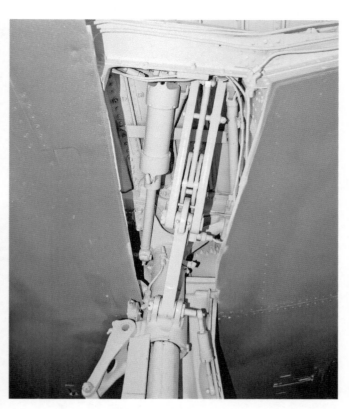

This closeup provides a good look at the details inside the outer section of the left gear well. The hydraulic piston and cylinder and the drag link are visible. During restoration of this F-80C, the piston for the hydraulic cylinder was painted white: however, it should be a shiny natural metal. (Kinzey)

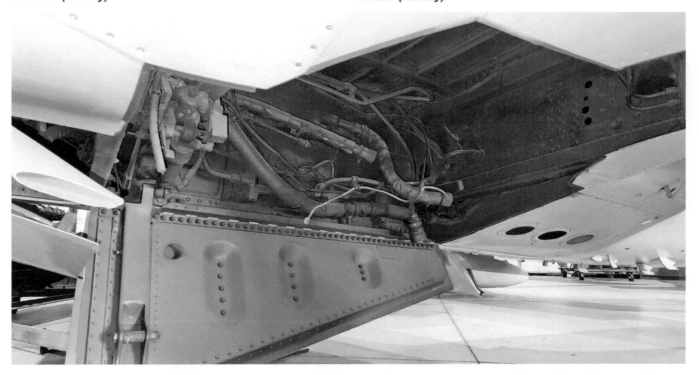

Hydraulic lines, wires, and other plumbing were located in the larger inboard section of the left landing gear. The tapered inboard door was hinged to the fuselage near the centerline. Note the IFF lights aft of the well. These were on early P-80s/F-80s. (Manning).

RIGHT MAIN LANDING GEAR DETAILS

Above and right: The right landing gear was simply a mirror image of the left. It is shown from the front in the photo above and from the inside in the photo at right. Again, the color of the struts and wheel wells would not be white on operational aircraft. The struts would be a steel or aluminum color, and the wells would be either Interior Green or silver. (Above, Noack; Right, Kinzey)

Above: This closeup shows the area at the base of the strut between the lower door and the wheel. The front of the brake assembly is visible with the hydraulic line attached to it. (Kinzey)

Right: Additional details of the right landing gear are illustrated in this photograph taken from behind. (Kinzey)

This photo shows the right landing gear from the inside and slightly to the front. The colors on this museum aircraft accurately reflect those used on early Shooting Stars. Later production aircraft usually would have the inner surfaces of the doors and the interior of the wells painted silver. (Manning)

Details inside the outer section of the right wheel well are revealed here. The drag strut, hydraulic cylinder, linkages, and brake lines are visible. This restored aircraft has the interior of the wells painted silver as they usually were on later Shooting Stars. (Kinzey)

This view looks up and slightly aft into the larger inboard section of the right gear well, and most of the inboard door is also visible. (Manning)

INTERNAL ARMAMENT DETAILS

The internal armament on all fighter versions of the P-80/F-80 consisted of six .50-caliber Browning machine guns mounted in the nose. The three guns and their ammunition boxes on the right side are visible in this photograph. Also note the radio gear installed at the aft end of the gun bay. Vintage color photographs indicate that the interior of the gun bay was painted Chromate Green on some aircraft and Zinc Chromate Yellow primer on others. The difference in colors may be attributable to repainting at maintenance depots. (Kinzey)

Armorers load .50-caliber ammunition into the ammo boxes of an F-80C assigned to the 80th Fighter Bomber Squadron of the 8th Fighter Bomber Group at Osan Air Base during the Korean War. Up to 300 rounds of ammunition could be loaded for each gun, providing a total of 1,800 rounds. The large panels on each side of the nose that covered the gun bay were much like the design used for the gun bays on Lockheed's P-38 Lightning during World War II. (NMUSAF)

All of the ammunition boxes have been removed from the gun bay in this photograph as armorers prepare to re-load them for this Shooting Star assigned to the 7th Fighter Bomber Squadron of the 49th Fighter Bomber Group. Again, note the radio gear at the aft end of the gun bay. (Menard Collection via NMUSAF)

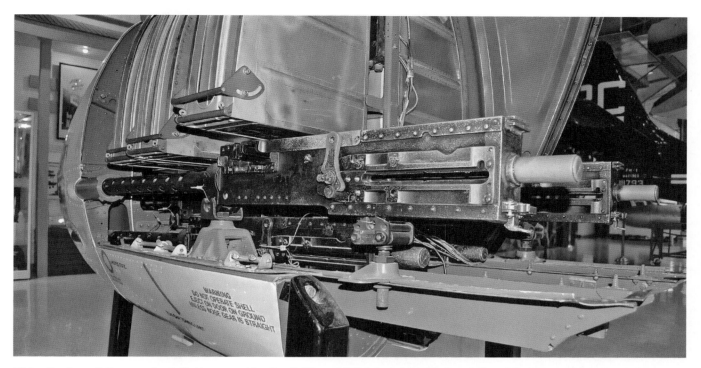

This display of the gun installation used in the F-80 and TV-1 is at the National Naval Aviation Museum aboard NAS Pensacola, Florida. It provides a good look at the details of the gun bay, except that the feed chutes between the ammunition boxes and the machine guns are not present. (Kinzey)

This close-up provides a good look at the mounts for the aft left gun on top and the center left gun below it. (Kinzey)

Each cover for the gun bay was attached to the fuselage at the top by three large hinges. Also note the support rod that held the cover in the open position. (Kinzey)

The mounting positions of all six machine guns are visible in this aft view. Note how the forward-most guns are mounted in a staggered position and that they are nearest the center of the compartment. This photograph also provides a good look at the shape of the ammunition boxes. (Kinzey)

PYLONS & EXTERNAL STORES DETAILS

EXTERNAL FUEL TANKS

The original specifications for the P-80 Shooting Star called for it to have the ability to carry external fuel tanks and bombs under the wing tips. The first type of fuel tank carried by the P-80/F-80 was a teardrop-shaped tank that held 165-gallons. It had a rounded nose and a tapered and pointed aft end. These two photographs show one style of this early tank flush-fitted to the wing tips. These tanks were made in both left and right configurations so that the refueling point could be on the outboard side of the tank. However, both left and right tanks could be mounted under either wing tip, and access to the refueling point was easy regardless of the mounting. (Both, Kinzey)

The original 165-gallon tanks were made by several different manufacturers and had some detail differences. On this tank, note the external ribs that ran vertically on the nose and aft sections where the left and right halves were joined together. As seen here, some tanks were mounted with a noticeable gap between the tank and the wing, and plumbing was visible in the gap. The fuel line and the air tubes are visible in the closeup at right. Part of the apparatus inside the wing tip for mounting stores required there to be a small bump or fairing on top of the wing tip near the leading edge. (Both, Kinzey)

This 165-gallon tank was made by Curtiss Wright, and it is different from the two seen above. In this case, there is a flush seam that runs horizontally around the tank where upper and lower halves were joined together. (NMUSAF)

The tank in this photograph is the same as the one in the center photos above. It has the external vertical ribbing on the nose and aft end of the tank. However, there is an aerodynamic fairing at the top where it mounts to the wing tip, leaving no gap and none of the plumbing exposed. (NMUSAF)

The second type of fuel tank to be carried under the wing tips was manufactured by Fletcher. It had a much more pointed nose than the original tanks, and it was made in three sections with the center section being cylindrical in shape. One is seen here under the right wing tip of Baird Martin's (to whom this book is dedicated) F-80C in Korea as the Shooting Star is being refueled. Note the open filler cap on the tank. (G. Balzer Collection)

The short range of the Shooting Star in Korea led to a modification of the Fletcher tank to increase the amount of fuel that could be carried. In most cases, two extra center sections were added to the tank, as seen on this F-80C assigned to the 80th Fighter Bomber Squadron. With these tanks, the total fuel capacity was increased by 220 gallons (110 gallons in each tank), thus significantly extending the range and loiter time of the aircraft. This modification had been evaluated unofficially in 1949, prior to the war, but it had never been approved. Once the war in Korea began, and with the F-80s having to operate from Japan in most of the early months, General Earle Partridge, the commanding general of the Fifth Air Force, authorized the use of these tanks. They became known as the Misawa tanks, because they allowed F-80Cs to operate more effectively from Misawa and other bases in Japan. However, care had to be taken while pulling "G" forces during maneuvers with the much heavier tanks when significant amounts of fuel remained in them. (G. Balzer Collection)

In some cases, only one center section was added to the standard Fletcher tank to increase the amount of fuel that could be carried. This became more practical as the F-80s began to operate from bases on the Korean peninsula. With only two center sections, the tanks did not have the severe "G" limits that the tanks with the three center sections did. However, the Misawa tanks with the three center sections were far more common during the Korean War. Here, ground crew personnel attach a tank with two center sections to the right wing tip of a Shooting Star. (NMUSAF)

While the standard Fletcher tanks and the tanks with the Misawa modifications with the extra center sections were used throughout the Korean War, a more permanent external tank with increased fuel capacity was developed and manufactured. It had a more rounded nose and a single large center section. An aerodynamic fairing was fitted between the tank and the wing tip. This was the last external fuel tank to be carried under the wing tips of the Shooting Star, and it became operational on F-80s during the Korean War. It was also used in the post-war years. One is seen here on an F-80A that was assigned to a training unit at Williams Air Force Base. (Menard Collection via NMUSAF)

The final external tank used on the wing tips of F-80s was similar in size to the Misawa tank with the three center sections, and it had a capacity of 230 gallons. However, it mounted directly on the wing tip, rather than under it. It also had a small fin on the outboard side at the aft end. One is seen here on the wing tip of an upgraded F-80B-5-LO, S/N 45-8490, assigned to the New Mexico ANG. The 0- in front of the last four digits of the serial number on the tail indicates that the aircraft is more than ten years old. This tank was also the most common one used on the T-33 trainer version of the Shooting Star and on the F-94 Starfire interceptors, although the early style 165-gallon tanks had initially been used on both of those aircraft. (Menard Collection via NMUSAF)

BOMBS

On the F-80C an additional hardpoint was under each wing to carry external stores. Bombs up to the 1,000-pound size could be loaded on pylons attached to these two hardpoints. External fuel tanks of the 75-gallon type could also be mounted. For most of the operational service of the F-80, the pylons were rectangular in shape, as seen in these two photographs. These were retrofitted to many F-80Bs during upgrades to F-80C standards. (Both, Kinzey)

Fairly late in the operational service of the Shooting Star, a slightly larger pylon with an angled leading edge was used on these two external hard points. (Both, Kinzey)

A small rack could be attached to the retractable stubs that were usually used to mount 5-inch rockets under each wing. With these racks in place, two small 100- or 250-pound bombs could be loaded under each wing to increase the bomb-carrying capability of the F-80C. (NMUSAF)

Above: Bombs could also be carried on the hardpoints under the wing tips. Here, armorers load 100-pound practice bombs under the right wing tip of an F-80A during the First Annual Gunnery Meet at Las Vegas Air Force Base, Nevada, on May 3, 1949. (Bell Collection)

Left: Bombs up to the 1,000-pound size could be loaded on the wing tip stations, giving the Shooting Star the ability to carry up to 4,000 pounds of bombs. Two 1,000-pound bombs are loaded under the right wing of this F-80C assigned to the 36th Fighter Bomber Squadron of the 8th Fighter Bomber Group in Korea. With this load, and no external fuel, the target had to be fairly close to the operating base. (G. Balzer Collection)

75-gallon fuel tanks were filled with napalm and used as fire bombs in Korea. Here, an F-80C retracts its landing gear as it takes off on a mission with two of these fire bombs loaded under the wings. Misawa fuel tanks are under the wing tips. (G. Balzer Collection)

5-INCH ROCKETS

Above: The flight manual for the F-80B and F-80C states that eight 5-inch rockets could be loaded under the wings in four pairs, as seen here on this F-80B that is being prepared for rocket-firing tests. However, photographs of rocket-armed F-80Cs in Korea always showed the rockets being loaded singly rather than in pairs. (NMUSAF)

Right: Two 5-inch rockets are loaded singly under the left wing of this Shooting Star. The rockets were mounted on stubs that retracted into the underside of the wing when not in use. (See the Wings Details section in this chapter.) Note that the aft mounting consisted of two small stubs attached to the two upper fins of the rocket. This arrangement differed from the mountings for 5-inch rockets on most other aircraft that consisted of two single mounts attached to the body of the rocket. (NMUSAF)

These two photos show airmen loading rockets on F-80Cs. The photo at left again reveals the unusual aft attachment for the rockets with the two small stubs being attached to the top fins on the rocket. Sometimes, the warheads were added after the rockets were in place under the wings. (Both, NMUSAF)

TAIL DETAILS

Right: Although the design of the vertical tail remained basically the same for all P-80/F-80 variants, there were some detail differences. On the early P-80As/F-80As, and all RF-80s, the pitot probe was high on the leading edge of the vertical tail, as seen on this early Shooting Star. But the pitot probe was soon moved to a position beneath the nose. The new L-shaped probe was retrofitted to existing fighter versions that had been delivered with the probe on the vertical tail; however, the RF-80As retained the probe on the tail due to the camera windows under the nose. P-80As and F-80As also initially had the wire antenna for the command radio that ran from the vertical tail, through a hole in the canopy, and into the cockpit where it attached behind the armored headrest. (Bell Collection)

Below left: This high-angle view of the F-80C on display at the USAF Armament Museum provides an excellent over-all look at the empennage of the Shooting Star. (Kinzey)

Below right: The F-80A at the Museum of Aviation at Warner Robins, Georgia, illustrates the updates that later changed the details of the vertical tail on F-80As and which would be standard on the subsequent fighter versions. The pitot probe is gone, and the wire antenna for the command radio has also been deleted. The black item on the leading edge of the fin cap is the AN/ARC-3 radio antenna. Directional control around the vertical axis was provided by a large rudder that spanned the entire height of the vertical stabilizer except for the fin cap at the top. A small fixed tab was on the trailing edge of the rudder; however, there was no movable trim tab. (Kinzey)

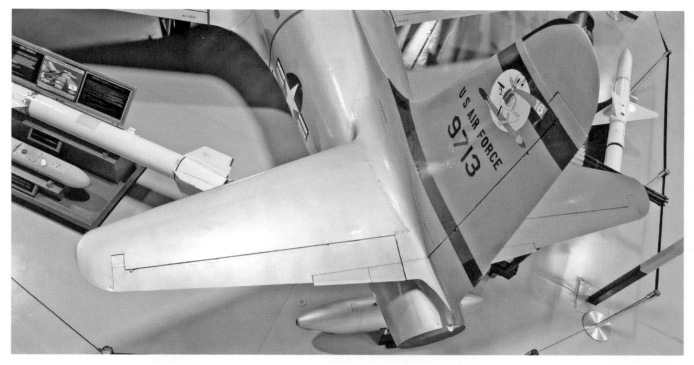

This high view provides a good look at the planform of the horizontal tails. Being an early subsonic jet fighter with a maximum airframe limit of .80 Mach, the Mach tuck phenomena, which plagued later jet fighters that approached and exceeded the speed of sound, was not really an issue for the Shooting Star. That problem resulted in what became known as the all-flying tail, but the F-80 retained the conventional fixed horizontal stabilizers and movable elevators that proved to be satisfactory for its maximum speed limitations. (Kinzey)

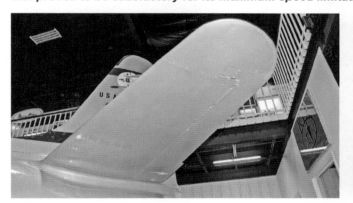

The underside of the left horizontal tail assembly is shown at left. The elevator spanned almost the entire horizontal stabilizer, and it had a counterbalance at the outboard end. At right is a closeup of the trim tab on the elevator with its actuator on the underside of the unit. (Both, Kinzey)

The right horizontal tail assembly was simply a mirror image of the left. Both elevators had trim tabs, and in both cases the actuators were on the underside of the elevator. An aerodynamic fairing under each horizontal tail assembly smoothed the airflow around it. (Both, Kinzey)

ENGINE DETAILS

All variants of the Shooting Star were powered by the J33 centrifugal flow turbojet engine that was produced by the Allison Division of General Electric. To gain access to the powerplant for maintenance or to change out the engine meant removing the entire tail section and opening up the top of the fuselage, as seen here on F-80A-1-LO, S/N 44-85262, while undergoing an engine change at Williams Air Force Base, Arizona. A special stand was used to remove the tail section, hold it while the engine was being worked on or changed out, then to rejoin it to the fuselage. (Menard Collection)

This photograph provides a good look at the removed tail section and the interior of the fuselage as the engine replacement is taking place. Note that the exhaust pipe remained mounted inside the tail section, rather than being attached to the engine. (Bell Collection)

A J33 engine is on display at the National Museum of Naval Aviation, and some of the engine has been cut away to reveal its interior components. (Kinzey)

Above: This rear view of the J33 that is on display at the National Museum of Naval Aviation provides a good look at the aft compressor blades (in yellow) and the flame holder and vanes (in red). (Kinzey)

Right: The engine accessories were on the front end of the J33, and details are visible here as an engine is unpacked in preparation for installation in a Shooting Star. Over the operational service of the F-80, the J33 was improved over several variants, some of which had water/ alcohol injection. They all were interchangeable, and as they became available, the later and more powerful and reliable versions of the engine were usually retrofitted to earlier aircraft. (Bell Collection)

MODELERS SECTION

A considerable number of scale models of the Shooting Star have been issued in all standard modeling scales from 1/144th through 1/32nd scale, although none of them are truly exceptional. In this photo, the OzMods 1/144th scale F-80B/C is up front to the left of center. Just behind it, from left to right, are the Airfix F-80C which has been backdated to a P-80A, the Gran Ltd. F-80C, and the Sword RF-80A, all in 1/72nd scale. Behind them is the classic Monogram F-80C in 1/48th scale which remains the best kit of the Shooting Star in any scale. (Kinzey)

Note: Each volume in the Detail & Scale Series has a Modelers Section in the back of the book where we discuss and review the injection-molded plastic kits of the subject aircraft. Resin kits will be included if they are the only options in a given scale or for a specific variant of the aircraft. All standard scales are included. Highlights, limitations, and recommendations are provided with respect to which kits in each scale are the best for the scale modeler. Modelers should compare the features of a kit to the detailed photographs in the book to determine how accurately and extensively they are represented. The modeler can then decide what, if any, work to undertake to enhance the appearance of the model.

GENERAL COMMENTS

Models of the P-80/F-80 Shooting Star have been released in all of the standard modeling scales from 1/144th through 1/32nd, although there has never been a truly outstanding kit in any scale. Some kits are quite old, having been initially released decades ago. And while each of the scales are represented, the number of kits in each are very limited. Of the kits that can be considered by the serious scale modeler, there has only been one kit in 1/144th scale, and while there have been three in 1/72nd scale, one is quite old and the other two were limited production kits that are no longer available. In 1/48th scale, the Monogram kit, initially released in 1977, remains the most accurate, but it had some fit problems and is no longer in production. Fortunately, it is easy to find on online auction sites and at model shows. The current HobbyBoss kits of the F-80 and RF-80 in 1/48th scale leave a lot to be desired when it comes to accuracy. In 1/32nd scale, only one kit has been released, although it has been issued under two different labels. It presents some challenges to build, but it can be completed

as a nice model if the modeler takes time to address its issues. Given the historical importance of the Shooting Star as the first jet fighter to enter operational service with the U. S. Air Force, we hope that better kits of it will be released in the future in all standard modeling scales.

OLDER KITS

When the Shooting Star became operational and then saw combat in the Korean War, injection molded plastic kits were in their infancy. Jet aircraft were all the rage at that time, and the P-80/F-80 was the subject of several older wood and paper kits, solid wood kits, and the new plastic models. Among the companies that produced the first P-80 models were Guillow's, Maircraft, Strombecker, and Comet. Trim Model Products released a small 1/96th scale plastic kit of a P-80 in 1957, and it was subsequently issued by Lindberg, Replikits, Sunil, and Necomisa. But the best known, and the one that would remain on the market the longest, was released by Lindberg in what was approximately 1/48th scale. Today, all of these older kits have value only to kit collectors, and they cannot be considered as buildable by serious scale modelers. Because of this, we will not review them here with the exception of the Lindberg kit. Because it has been released relatively recently, we are including some brief review comments about it in this OLDER KITS subsection.

Originally released by O-lin in 1947 and again in 1948, this kit initially appeared under the Lindberg label in 1953 while the war in Korea was in its final year. It has been released numerous times since then, with the most recent issue being in 2018 in a combination kit with an F-94C Starfire. It was also released in 1960 by a company called Sunil. Like most kits from the early-to-mid 1950s, including the other models of the more serious model building. We tried this with one of the Lindberg kits, but the completed project was disappointing, because the inaccuracies in shape and outline are so severe that, even as a desk stand model, they detracted from its overall appearance.

When it comes to the Lindberg kit, leave it and the other old Shooting Star models to the kit collectors.

1/144th SCALE MODEL

OzMods F-80B/C

The Australian company OzMods has released a nice kit of the Shooting Star in 1/144th scale. The shape and outline of the kit accurately represents the real thing. The model features recessed panel lines and details, although not all features are represented. Most notably, there is no representation of the six machine guns. The parts do not have pins, holes, tabs, or slots to assist in alignment during assembly, so extra care is needed to make sure everything goes together correctly. Fit is generally good, although a little filling and sanding is required, most notably where the wing joins the fuselage on the underside. Some parts have a very small amount of flash that is easily removed. Construction is straightforward with only one issue: some thin plastic card needs to be added inside the main gear wells to avoid a hollow look up into the fuselage. The nose gear doors come as one part and need to be cut apart if the landing gear is to be displayed in the extended position. But the nose gear doors are also a bit on the thick side, and in building our review sample, we replaced the kit doors with new ones made from thin plastic card.

The cockpit is quite good for such a small model and fea-

One of the earliest plastic model kits of the Shooting Star was in roughly 1/48th scale from Lindberg. It had numerous and very obvious shape and outline inaccuracies, and it lacked detailing. Therefore, it cannot be recommended for today's serious scale modelers. As a nostalgic build, the author built this one in a gear-up configuration to be used as a very basic desk stand model. Decals were from a Microscale sheet for a P-80A-1-LO named "Rhapsody in Rivets" that was flown by the commander of the 412th Fighter Group in 1946. (Kinzey)

Shooting Star, the Lindberg kit suffered from significant inaccuracies and a lack of detailing. It was based on an early P-80A and featured scribing for the landing/taxi light on the nose that was present on the earliest production P-80As. The surface detailing was recessed, but it was incomplete and inaccurate. There wasn't even any represention of the two speed brakes under the fuselage. Rivets were present, but they were light and easily removed. The wings and the horizontal tails were very thin, so the horizontal tails could easily be bent. Neither the wings nor the horizontal tails had an airfoil shape to them.

The fuselage also had major shape problems with the nose section in particular being noticeably wrong. The engine inlets were incorrect in shape, and there was a recessed area in front of each intake that was not present on the real aircraft. The plate inside each inlet was also incorrect in shape, and it did not extend forward of the inlet enough. The boundary layer bleed air vents on each inlet were not represented.

Detailing was also lacking. The cockpit consisted only of a tub with a very poor seat, a pilot figure, a control column, and an instrument panel. The best that could be said for these parts was that they were generic in nature, rather than being any real representation of the actual cockpit. The landing gear was very crude and simplistic, and it did not come close to representing the real thing.

At times we build older kits as gear-up desk stand models where we do not consider accuracy as important as it is for

The smallest of the Shooting Star models is this 1/144th scale kit from OzMods in Australia. This is a very good kit, although some improvements can easily be made by the builder to enhance the finished model as described in the text. Bert Kinzey used the OzMods kit to build this model of an F-80B-1-LO from the 22nd Fighter Squadron of the 36th Fighter Group. This is one of the decal options provided in the kit. (Kinzey)

tures a tub, seat, instrument panel, and control column. Once painted, it is quite sufficient if the canopy is attached in the closed position, and a little extra detailing by the modeler can result in a cockpit that deserves to have the canopy positioned in the open position to show the details. Plastic and vacu-formed canopies are included in the kit.

Both 165-gallon and the last type of underwing tip tanks are provided as options, but there are no bombs or rockets included. Plastic card can be used to add pylons, and bombs can be obtained from a weapons set or another 1/144th scale kit, if the modeler wants to add some external armament.

The decal sheet provides two options. One is for a P-80A assigned to the 1st Fighter Group. The second is for an F-80B assigned to the 22nd Fighter Squadron of the 36th Fighter Group. The decal sheet includes the anti-glare panel, walk-ways for the wings, markings for the fueling caps, and the NO STEP markings with red outlines for the top of the flaps.

Overall, this is a very nice 1/144th scale model, and we recommend it.

1/72nd SCALE MODELS

Airfix, MPC, and Airfix/Lodela F-80C

First released in 1973, the Airfix F-80C is still available today. Over the years, it has been released and rereleased several times under the Airfix, MPC, and Airfix/Lodela labels. While the kit represents an F-80C, it is easy to backdate it to an F-80B or even one of the earliest P-80As. Being more than a half-century old, the kit isn't up to today's standards of accuracy and detailing, but with some effort, a reasonably good model of the Shooting Star can be built from it. Since it remains in production as of the release date of this publication, it is much easier to find than the better but limited production Sword kits in 1/72nd scale.

The shape and outline are generally good, although the nose appears to be a little too narrow. Surface detailing is in the form of fine raised panel lines with heavier recessed lines that represent the control surfaces.

Cockpit details include a tub with side consoles that are a bit too narrow, and the rudder pedals are molded on the floor. The seat is poor and too wide, so replacing it with an after-market resin seat is best. The seat represents the ejection seat found in the F-80B and the F-80C, so if a P-80A/F-80A is being built, a fixed seat needs to be made from scratch. The instrument panel has inaccurate raised instruments represented as discs. A control column rounds out the details for the interior of the cockpit. The canopy is one clear piece, but it is a simple matter to cut it apart from the windscreen and display it in the open position. It represents the later electrically-operated canopy; however, modifying it to represent the earlier manu-ally-operated unit is easy. The landing/taxi lights to go on the nose gear strut are also included as a single clear part.

There are some accuracy issues including a gun camera that is too small inside the right intake. The pylons for the bombs are too long, causing the leading edge to be too close to the leading edge of the wing. Accordingly, the pylons need to be shortened. Bombs are provided to go on the pylons, but there are no rockets, and the retracted rocket stubs are not even etched into the plastic on the underside of the wings. Both the early 165-gallon tanks and the late-style underwing tanks are provided to go under the wing tips; however, the Mi-sawa-type tanks with their distinctive center sections are not included. The pitot probe is the L-shaped type mounted under the nose. To build an early F-80, this should be removed, and a thin plastic rod or pin should be used to represent the probe on the leading edge of the vertical stabilizer.

The nose gear strut must be glued into place before the fuselage halves are joined together, and this makes things a little awkward for the rest of the assembly process. Two types of nose gear wheels are provided. There is some detailing in the wheel wells, but it is far from complete. There are no sepa-rate parts for the retraction links for the nose and main landing gear. Instead, these are molded into the wells. Likewise, there are no actuators for the two speed brakes.

Fit is generally good with a couple of exceptions. The wing-to-fuselage joint on top of the wings is poor and will re-quire some filling and sanding. Another place that needs some attention is where the base of the vertical tail meets the fuse-lage on the right side.

The first F-80 kit to be released in 1/72nd scale was from Airfix, and it is still available today. While it shows its age and is not up to today's standards in fit, accuracy, and detailing, it can still be used to build an acceptable model of the Shooting Star. The author used the Airfix kit to build these two models. The one on the left was backdated to a P-80A in the original gray paint scheme and named "Stormy." The one on the right is an F-80C in the markings of the aircraft flown by Lt. Russell J. Brown of the 16th Fighter Interceptor Squadron when he shot down a MiG-15 on November 8, 1950, in what is believed to be the first jet-on-jet aerial victory in history. Note the kill marking on the fuselage next to the cockpit. (Kinzey)

It can be difficult to find the better but out of production Sword F-80 kit in 1/72nd scale, so until a manufacturer comes out with a new Shooting Star in this popular scale that is up to today's standards in accuracy and detailing, many modelers who want to add this important aircraft to their collection will have to use the Airfix kit. While it certainly is not optimum, some extra detailing and correcting of some easy to fix inaccuracies can result in a reasonably good model of any fighter version of the Shooting Star.

Gran Ltd. & Eastern Express F-80C

The Russian manufacturer, Gran Ltd., issued a 1/72nd scale kit of the F-80C in 1990, and it was subsequently issued under the Eastern Express label. A second release by Gran Ltd. was made sometime after 2000, but the company has since gone out of business, and these kits under either label are rather difficult to find. In all three cases, the plastic is the same, with only the box art and decals being changed from one issue to the next.

The model appears to have been copied to a considerable extent from the Airfix kit, but it is not a direct clone. There are some differences. For example, the vertical tail is part of the right fuselage half, while the Airfix kit has the vertical tail as part of the left fuselage half. This kit also has the option of positioning the flaps in the lowered position, while the Airfix kit does not. There are some other minor differences, but otherwise the kits are very similar.

The molding of details is not as fine or sharp as in most kits. Surface scribing is in the form of very fine raised lines with recessed lines for the control surfaces. The panel lines are incomplete, with some major details not represented. For example, there are no trim tabs on the elevators, or the left aileron. The right aileron is missing the fixed tab. There is some flash on several parts that will need to be removed before assembly, as will some of the rather heavy points where the parts are attached to the sprues.

Cockpit detailing includes a tub with side consoles, instrument panel, control column, and ejection seat. The seat is rather crude and should be replaced with an aftermarket seat. Once completed, the cockpit is covered by a single-piece windscreen and canopy. A second clear part provides the lenses for the landing/taxi lights that go on the nose gear strut.

The parts go together reasonably well with no major fit problems. However, there are noticeable gaps at the inboard end of each flap well and also inside the main gear wells. These are not really fit problems, rather they are actually short shots for the wheel wells and poor engineering for the flap wells. We used some very thin plastic card to fill in the openings at the inboard end of each flap well, and a little putty filled in the gaps inside the main gear wells.

The landing gear is rather fragile, and care must be taken not to break the parts. This is particularly true of the nose gear which must be added when the fuselage halves are joined together. The modeler must be careful not to break it during the rest of the construction process. There are no actuation struts for the gear, and adding these from thin plastic rod or pins will not only enhance the appearance of the model, it will also strengthen the gear assemblies. There is some detailing inside the wells, although it is simplified and not really accurate. Only the top of the nose gear well is provided. The sides are simply open to the inside of the forward fuselage. The two speed brakes come as separate parts, but the actuators are represented as rods rather than the correct V shape. The L-shaped pitot probe is included to go under the nose, and an exhaust pipe is provided to go in the aft fuselage.

External stores include two 500-pound bombs and their pylons to go under the wings, and both the original 165-gallon fuel tanks and the late-style extended tanks are provided to go under the wing tips, but as with the Airfix kit, the Misawa tanks with their distinctive center sections are not included. If the bombs are to be used, the holes for the pylons must be drilled out by the modeler before the wings are assembled.

With some work to clean up the parts, this model can be built to about the same level as the Airfix kit, but we rate the Airfix kit as being better when it comes to the molding of the parts. This factor, along with the fact that the Airfix kit is still readily available, makes the Airfix kit the better choice between the two, but neither of these kits is as good as the Sword kits that are reviewed next.

Sword F-80 & RF-80 Shooting Stars

Between 2009 and 2019, Sword released several kits of the Shooting Star, including kits of the P-80A/P-80B, the F-80C, and the RF-80C. Different parts were provided as options to build these variants. A clear part for the upper nose allows the modeler to build an early P-80A with the landing/

A lesser-known 1/72nd scale kit of the F-80C was released by the Russian company Gran Ltd. It has also been issued under the Eastern Express label. While it is very similar to the Airfix kit, it has the added feature of being able to drop the flaps. This limited-run kit is not as sharply molded as the Airfix and Sword kits, and it is very difficult to find one. The author used the Gran Ltd. kit and backdated it to an F-80A to build this model of a Shooting Star from the 56th Fighter Group. (Kinzey)

Sword has also released several limited-run kits of the Shooting Star in 1/72nd scale. Overall, they are better than the Airfix kit; however, they are no longer generally available, although they can be found at online auction sites and model shows. Paul Boyer used the F-80C kit from Sword to build this model of a Shooting Star named "Kansas Tornado" from the 16th Fighter Interceptor Squadron that saw service during the Korean War. (Boyer)

taxi lights in that position, and a solid plastic part is provided as an option to represent the radome that covers the AN/ARN-6 radio compass loop antenna for all subsequent fighter versions. Both the original pitot probe to go on the leading edge of the vertical tail on early P-80As/F-80As and the later small L-shaped one to go under the nose are provided. All of the optional parts come in each of the kits, and the instructions tell the modeler which ones to use for the variant being built. Since all of the kits of the fighter versions were basically the same, the comments in this review apply to all of them. Additional comments are included to cover the RF-80 kit. All were limited-run kits that are no longer in production except for the RF-80 kit, which was still available from retailers as of press time for this book. However, it is expected that this kit will also become unavailable from retailers very shortly. While they can be found at online auction sites and model shows, the relatively small production numbers for each kit makes them more difficult to find than many other kits, and therefore the prices are often rather high. However, these are the best kits of the Shooting Star that have been produced to date in 1/72nd scale.

Because they are all limited production kits, there are no pins and holes or tabs and slots to assist with lining up the parts during assembly, so care must be taken when glue is added and the parts are joined together to ensure that they are properly aligned. Resin parts are included for the interior of the wheel wells and the ejection seat, but remember that the ejection seat is not correct for the early P-80A/F-80A or the RF-80A. The early teardrop-shaped 165-gallon tanks and the late-style extended tanks are provided to go under the

wing tips. However, as with the Airfix and Gran Ltd. kits, the distinctive Misawa tanks are not included. Interestingly, the instructions show the longer tanks as the Misawa type, but the plastic on the sprues represents the last style of underwing tip tanks that were used on Shooting Stars. This means that no 1/72nd scale F-80 kit provides the Misawa tanks with either two or three center sections, nor is the original Fletcher tank with the single short center section provided. Bombs and pylons are also included as external stores.

The landing gear is better detailed than that found in the Airfix kit with the retraction linkages included as separate parts; however, the instructions show the nose gear drag strut going in backwards.

Surface detailing is well done and is in the form of recessed panel lines. One minor inaccuracy is that there is no representation of the gun camera in the right intake. All shapes and outlines are accurate and are better than the Airfix kit. Fit is generally good, but some filling and sanding between the wing and fuselage will be required, particularly where the rear of the wing assembly meets the fuselage.

Clear parts include separate parts for the windscreen and canopy, making it easy to display the canopy in the closed or opened positions. However, the landing/taxi lights to go on the nose gear strut are provided as a single resin part, making it necessary to represent the lenses with silver paint.

Building the Sword RF-80 kit is a bit more involved than Sword's kits of the fighter versions of the Shooting Star. This is their F-80C kit with three clear plastic parts to build the photo reconnaissance nose. So plastic surgery is required to re-

Sword also released a kit that allowed the modeler to build an RF-80. However, this release was simply the unchanged original F-80C kit with the additional parts for the photo reconnaissance nose. The modeler had to cut off the gun nose of the F-80C kit with a razor saw and then add the three parts that comprised the camera nose. The parts for the camera nose were molded in clear plastic, so they could be painted, leaving the camera windows clear. The author used the RF-80 kit from Sword to build this photo recon Shooting Star that had an unusual camouflage scheme and the markings of the 45th Tactical Reconnaissance Squadron at Kimpo Air Base, Korea, in 1952. Photos of the actual aircraft appear in the Korean War chapter of this book. (Kinzey)

move the gun nose of the F-80C and then replace it with the clear plastic recon nose. Care must be taken to get the new nose lined up correctly before it is joined to the fuselage. It can be quite noticeable on the finished model if it is off by even a couple of degrees. By painting the inside of the recon nose black and painting the outside the color of the aircraft, a nice effect can be achieved, and this is better than having a solid plastic nose with clear windows. The adventuresome modeler can even take it a step further and add scratch-built cameras inside the nose. In building our review sample, we simply put weight in the nose, so the model would sit properly on its landing gear. Only a representation of the camera lens was added to be seen in the large oblique window on the left side. For the RF-80A, the ejection seat should not be used. It is relatively simple to make a fixed seat using plastic card. The camera control panel can also be added to the instrument panel in the cockpit using thin plastic card. Simply refer to the photo of it in the RF-80 section of the Shooting Star Variants chapter.

One of the nicest features of the RF-80 kit is the decal sheet which includes six different options for markings. Overall, we recommend the Sword kits as the best option to build a Shooting Star in 1/72nd scale.

1/48th SCALE MODELS

Monogram, Bandai/Monogram, Monogram/Necomisa, Hasegawa/Monogram, Hasegawa, & Hasegawa/Revell/Monogram F-80C

Although some older models of the Shooting Star were issued in 1/48th scale, or something close to it, most notably the Lindberg kit covered above, the first quality kit of the F-80 in this popular scale was initially released by Monogram in 1977. It has since been issued numerous times by Monogram and also under the Bandai/Monogram, Monogram/Necomisa, Hasegawa/Monogram, Hasegawa, and Hasegawa/Revell/Monogram labels. The most recent issue was in 2011 under the Monogram label. Although the age of the kit is approaching the half-century mark, it clearly remains the most accurate model of the F-80C in 1/48th scale, and it can be argued that it is the most accurate Shooting Star in any scale.

In 1977, Monogram was making an effort to add detailing to its models, moving well beyond the toy-like features of plas-

tic models from the previous decade. For this kit, Monogram included the option of opening up the left side of the gun bay with nice details of the machine guns, ammunition boxes, and other gear inside. The shortcoming in this area was that there were no hinges on the door that covered the gun bay. The modeler was simply supposed to glue the edge of the top of the door to the top edge of the gun bay on the fuselage. This was probably to allow the door to fit easily if it was to be assembled in the closed position. Since these hinges are rather large and noticeable, and because they would add to the strength of the joint between the door and the fuselage in the open position, while building our review sample, we made all three hinges out of thin plastic card, referring to the photos in the details chapter of this publication. Additionally, we used a piece of thin plastic rod to represent the brace that held the door in the open position.

The aft fuselage and tail section could be built separately from the rest of the fuselage, and a stand was provided on which to place it. This revealed the J33 engine that was included to be attached to the main fuselage. However, Monogram oversimplified this option. They had the tail pipe attached to the engine, but the tail pipe actually remained inside of the tail section when it was removed to provide access to the engine. Further, the top of the main fuselage section would be opened when the engine was being replaced, and Monogram did not provide parts to do this. What the real thing looked like can be studied in the photos provided in the Engine Details section of the Shooting Star Details chapter of this publication. If a modeler wanted to have the tail section separate from the fuselage, the tail pipe should be cut off from the engine and glued in place inside the tail section. Some detailing inside the exhaust area of the engine would also have to be added to represent the vanes and the + shaped flame holder. This would represent the tail section being removed from the aircraft, but before the top panel would be opened to gain access to the forward accessory end of the engine. Even with the tail section joined to the fuselage, the stand provided can still be placed under the aircraft to add to the presentation of the finished model. Regardless of how the tail pipe is used, there are some large ejector pin markings inside the pipe that should be removed.

Being a kit that originally dates from the 1970s, the surface detailing is mostly raised panel lines with recessed lines representing the control surfaces. The flaps are separate

The Monogram F-80C kit in 1/48th scale dates back to 1977, and it has been released numerous times since then. While it is no longer in production, it is considered to be a classic, and it can easily be found at online auction sites and model shows. It remains the most accurate Shooting Star model in 1/48th scale to this day. Monogram included detailing in the form of an open left side to the gun bay and a tail section that could be positioned away from the model on a stand to reveal the engine. The author built one of the early releases of the kit to represent an F-80C from the 35th Fighter Bomber Squadron of the 8th Fighter Bomber Group in Korea. (Kinzey)

pieces that can be assembled in the lowered position. But the detailing is accurate and complete. Even if care is taken when sanding out seams, some of the surface detailing will inevitably be removed, but it is rather easy to rescribe it where necessary.

The cockpit has some good detailing, and the ejection seat is a good representation of the real thing, although we used a resin replacement in our review build. However, there are some improvements that are needed. First, the instrument panel is too far up under the coaming, and it needs to be repositioned farther aft on the cockpit tub to correct this issue. The control column is too tall and needs to be shortened. There is no representation of the throttle, but since it was simply the shape of a cylindrical handle, it is a simple matter to make one from thin plastic rod. Another enhancement we added involved cutting off the solid plastic part that represents the reflector glass of the gun sight and replacing it with a very thin piece of clear plastic sheet. We also used plastic card to add the rails behind the seat that were part of the mechanism that moved the canopy between the open and closed positions. That area was left bare by Monogram. This is fine if the canopy is assembled in the closed position, but these parts are very noticeable if it is displayed in the open position.

The landing gear is excellent, and the main gear struts even have the brake lines represented. There is nice detailing inside the wheel wells, and the representation of the wheels is quite good. We did not see a need to replace them with aftermarket resin wheels and tires.

External stores include two 1,000-pound bombs and two 75-gallon fuel tanks to go on the underwing pylon. The 75-gallon tanks were used as napalm fire bombs in Korea. A prob-

lem with the bombs is that they assemble to the pylon with the fins in the + position, and this is incorrect. They should be in the X position instead. We simply filled in the holes in the bombs and redrilled new holes to obtain the correct alignment before adding them to the model. Two types of underwing tip tanks are provided, and these include the original 165-gallon tanks with the aerodynamic fairings between the tank and the wing. The other tank that is included is the Fletcher tank with its single cylindrical center section. Unfortunately, there are no rockets provided, nor are the retractable mounts for the rockets scribed into the underside of the wings, but these are shortcomings found in all kits of the Shooting Star.

This kit is well known for its fit problems, and they certainly exist. However, we found by taking our time, being extra careful with dry fitting and making adjustments before parts were glued in place, and taking care in filling and sanding, these were overcome with relatively little difficulty. We were even able to retain the attachment points for the JATO bottles under the fuselage right next to the joint where the wing assembly meets the tail section. The one place that required some extra work was the open area at the inboard end of each flap well where it meets the fuselage. We used some plastic card and some modeling putty to fill these in.

While this kit shows its age and can use some extra detailing in the cockpit, it remains the most accurate F-80 kit in 1/48th scale, and arguably it is the most accurate Shooting Star in any scale. Monogram got all of the shapes and outlines right on the money. Since many of the issues of this kit are easily found at online auction sites and model shows at reasonable prices, we recommend them as the best choice for building an F-80 in 1/48th scale.

HobbyBoss F-80A, RF-80, & F-80C

Beginning in 2013, HobbyBoss released 1/48th scale kits of the F-80A, RF-80A, and finally the F-80C. As of the release date of this publication, all three were still in production and available from retailers. The F-80A and F-80C kits are very similar with some optional parts to build either version, and the RF-80A has different parts to build the photo recon variant of the Shooting Star. Our review comments generally apply to all three kits, and we will provide additional information about the RF-80.

The biggest problem with the HobbyBoss Shooting Stars concerns inaccuracies in shapes, both in general and for specific parts. One of the noticeable problems with the finished model is that the air inlets are oversize, being much too large, and not tapered correctly with the correct rounded leading edge. The bleed air vents on each inlet are also too big. Additionally, features common to one variant are represented on another variant that did not have them. For example, the panel on the vertical tail for the AN/ARA-8A radio antenna is represented in all of the kits, but they were not present on P-80As/F-80As, F-80Cs, or RF-80As. What makes this even more interesting is that HobbyBoss put the panel on the right side of the tail but not the left! It should be on both sides for the F-80B and on neither side for the other variants. The mast antenna under the forward fuselage is included in the F-80C kit, although that variant did not have that antenna. Ejection seats are provided for all variants, but they are not correct for the P-80A/F-80A or the RF-80A.

Another very noticeable inaccuracy involves the flaps. These are separate pieces that allow the modeler to position them in the lowered position. However, HobbyBoss got them wrong. The trailing edge of the upper wing surface on the actual aircraft is actually part of the flap, but the kit parts don't represent this. They have that part of the flap molded integral with the top part of each wing. The simplest remedy to fix this inaccuracy is to glue the flaps to the wings in the closed position. To accurately show the flaps in the lowered position, the modeler needs to cut off the part of the trailing edge of the upper wing section along the scribed panel line and glue that to the trailing edge of the flap.

Additional inaccuracies involve the external fuel tanks to go under the wing tips. The early 165-gallon tanks are noticeably too large and bulbous in shape. Further, there is no representation of the noticeable filler caps on them. The other option is for the Misawa tanks, and there are problems with them as well. While they are close to the correct size and shape for the Misawa tank with the three center sections, there are no scribed lines to indicate the center sections, and again there is no representation of the filler cap. But most noticeable is that their locating holes have the mount to the wing tips too far aft, and this causes the tanks to extend way too far forward of the wing tip and too little aft of the wing. If used, these tanks should be mounted correctly on the wing tip, being centered under it. However, they are the only Misawa type tanks in 1/48th scale kits.

Other external stores include two 500-pound bombs and two 75-gallon fuel tanks that were used as napalm in Korea. But like the tanks that go under the wing tips, these are also missing the filler caps which were very noticeable details. No rockets are provided to go under the wings, nor are the retractable mounts for rockets engraved on the undersurface of the wings.

HobbyBoss and their sister label, Trumpeter, are notorious for providing engines in their models that will be completely invisible once the model is assembled, and these Shooting Star kits are no exception. Like the Monogram kit, HobbyBoss has provided a simplified engine to go inside the aft fuselage. But unlike the Monogram kit, there is no option to build the tail section separate from the rest of the fuselage. While the tail section is molded as separate parts, there is no interior detailing that would be important for such an option, and there is no stand on which to place it. All the engine parts do is to add weight to the rear of the model, thus requiring more weight in the nose to counterbalance it.

Interestingly, HobbyBoss also includes some radio gear in the nose section, but there are no guns or ammunition boxes. Only short tubes go inside the openings to represent muzzles of the gun barrels. There is no option for an open gun bay, so the equipment at the aft end of the bay will not be visible at all when the model is completed. Just use this area to add enough weight to have the model sit properly on its landing gear when it is finished.

Cockpit detailing is generally good, and an ejection seat is provided in all of the kits. This needs to be replaced in the F-80A and RF-80A kits, because they did not have ejection seats. Etched metal parts are included for the seat belts and shoulder harness, but an overall better option would be to use an aftermarket resin seat. Decals are provided for the instrument panel and the left side of the cockpit. No throttle is in-

The HobbyBoss F-80C in 1/48th scale was used by Stan Parker to build this model of a Shooting Star from the 80th Fighter Bomber Squadron. Named "The Spirit of HOBO," this F-80C flew the 50,000th sortie flown by the 8th FBG in Korea. While the HobbyBoss kit has better fit overall than the Monogram kit, it still has its problems, and it has some serious and obvious accuracy issues. The noticeably oversized and incorrectly shaped engine inlets are apparent in this photo, as are the inaccurate 165-gallon fuel tanks which are too large and bulbous in shape. (Parker)

Stan Parker also built the RF-80 kit from HobbyBoss in 1/48th scale. Like the HobbyBoss F-80C, this kit also has accuracy issues and omissions of obvious details that must be corrected. Rather surprisingly, the window for the right oblique camera is not represented at all, nor are the three windows for the vertical cameras under the nose. The very poor nose gear wheel is evident in this photo. Unfortunately, it is the only kit of an RF-80 in 1/48th scale. HobbyBoss has the Misawa type tanks mounted much too far forward under the wing tips, but Stan Parker corrected that error when building this model for review. (Parker)

cluded, but this can easily be made from thin plastic rod.

The landing gear has some problems. While the main wheels and tires are acceptable, the nose wheel doesn't look much like either of the ones used on F-80s. The interiors of the wheel wells have some scribed detailing, and some small parts that are glued into the main wheel wells provide additional details. The struts are fairly well represented and the main struts include the brake lines. A clear part provides the landing/taxi lights that fit on the nose gear strut. The speed brakes are also separate pieces that can be assembled in the extended position, and the actuators are provided for them.

In addition to the clear part for the landing/taxi lights, other clear parts include the windscreen, the later-style canopy, the navigation lights to go on the wing tips, the reflector glass for the gunsight, and the clear part that is used for the early landing/taxi lights as found on the early production P-80As.

Fit is generally good, but there are several places that will require some filling and sanding. One problem area involves the horizontal stabilizers. Each horizontal stabilizer is made from two pieces; an upper half and a lower half. These are noticeably too thick and will require some sanding. This will remove the surface detailing which will have to be rescribed. The cockpit, inlet splitter plates, and the nose gear well are all a delicate fit that must be added inside the fuselage before the halves are joined together. Care must be taken to ensure that they are all properly in place or the two forward fuselage halves will not fit together properly.

The RF-80A kit has some additional accuracy problems of its own. First, it only has the left side window. The camera windows on the right side of the nose and under the nose are not included, nor is there any surface scribing to represent these windows. The modeler must cut out the opening for each of the windows and make clear parts to fit in them. A simpler, but far less desirable, solution would be to use black decals to represent the missing windows.

Another issue with the RF-80A is that HobbyBoss would have the modeler use the gunsight in this variant, but RF-80As did not have the gunsight.

With all of the very noticeable inaccuracies with the HobbyBoss kits, we do not recommend them. If a modeler wants to build a fighter variant of the Shooting Star in 1/48th scale, he would be much better off to find a Monogram kit and use that as a starting point. The Misawa style tanks from the HobbyBoss kit could be used with a Monogram kit as long as they were mounted correctly under the wing tips. If an RF-80A is to be built, the modeler is stuck with starting with the HobbyBoss kit, but much work will be needed to correct the inaccuracies and add the missing camera windows. Fixing the noticeably incorrect shape of the engine inlets would be problematic. While some inaccuracies can be fixed, correcting the inlets would be very difficult.

Stan Parker contributed to this review.

1/32nd SCALE MODEL

Czech Model and Special Hobby F-80C

NOTE: Because the Czech Model (also released by Special Hobby) F-80C in 1/32nd scale is a very difficult and challenging kit to build, we have asked master modeler, Gil Hodges, to not only review it, but to also offer valuable suggestions that will assist any modeler who wants to build this kit. These recommendations are based on Gil's experience in building this kit that resulted in the excellent model that is pictured with this review.

The Czech Models F-80C in 1/32nd scale has also been released under the Special Hobby label with a nice decal sheet with different options for markings and more compact instructions being the only significant changes. Being a limited-run kit, it doesn't have locating pins and holes for the main assemblies, the plastic tends to be overly thick in places, it has ejection pin marks that interfere with fit and need to be removed, and the engineering doesn't work as well as the designers intended. On the plus side, it has some excellent resin detail parts, colored PE parts for the cockpit's main instrument panel, and a superb decal sheet with a choice of colorful markings that go on very well. The instruction sheet is well illustrated and easy to understand; however, you can't really follow it and get good results.

The kit consists of about seventy-five gray plastic parts, a dozen well done injected clear parts, eighteen resin cast detail parts, and six PE parts. The surface detailing is good with recessed scribing. The modeler has a choice between two types of external tanks for the wingtips, two types of wingtip position lights, as well as a couple of wheel style choices between the

Gil Hodges overcame the serious fit and alignment problems of the Czech Model F-80C kit in 1/32nd scale to produce this excellent model of a Shooting Star named "STRIP 'N' STARE" that was assigned to the 25th Fighter Interceptor Squadron of the 51st Fighter Interceptor Group. Gil explains how to overcome the fit and alignment problems in his review of the kit. (Hodges)

plastic and resin tires provided. Two 500-pound bombs are the only external armament provided. The speed brakes are separate parts and designed and detailed to be assembled in the open position. However, the flaps are molded in the up position. The only obvious items missing in the kit are the retraction scissors for the nose gear well doors and the inner main gear door actuators.

The fit of the parts ranges from good, to marginal, to poor. In general, the smaller parts fit together well. The larger assemblies are problematic and require a lot of test fitting, adjusting, and manipulation to achieve good results. The biggest problems to be conquered are the fit of the intakes to the fuselage, the fit of the intake trunks to the inside of the intakes, the lack of dihedral in the wing, and the fit of the wing to the fuselage. I heartily recommend NOT following the kit instruction sequences and deviating in the following ways to correct these problems and get the best fit.

Before the fuselage halves are glued together, the intake bleed air ramps and the intakes themselves need to be glued into and onto their fuselage halves. This allows you to work from the inside and the outside to get them to fit. I also recommend leaving out the resin fuselage bleed air vents on the tops of the intakes until after you've sanded the intakes on the fuselage, lest they be obliterated. Try to "drop fit" them into place after the sanding is done to better preserve them.

Czech Models molded the interior intake ducting as a large "Y" assembly which is intended to be glued to the wing bottom

and then fit neatly up to the rear of the intakes when the wing is added. It simply doesn't work! The mouths of the intake trunk do not align well with the intakes, and they will interfere with the fit of the wing to the fuselage. The solution is to cut the Y apart, making two separate intake ducts. Then, each one can be individually fitted to its intake, pressing and twisting to get the smoothest transition and fit. Note that the outer edges of the intake ducts inside the fuselage may still need some grinding and trimming to keep them from hitting against the tops of the main wheel wells and inhibiting the fit of the wing. Thinning down the top inner edges of the main wheel wells in the wing bottom may also be needed to get clearance between the two of them.

One of the more trying problems is that the wing, as molded, is too flat; lacking the proper dihedral. The limited-run nature of the molding in between the main wheel wells, with the extra plastic there, makes it difficult to try to "bend" the wing in the center to give the wing the correct dihedral. What is needed is to grind out all of that plastic between the main gear wells with a motor tool and also remove the plastic that spans the front and rear of the bottom wing center sections. That will give the bottom wing the flex needed to make the next step work.

The tops of the outer main wheel wells are separate parts. They can aid in setting some dihedral on the bottom wing by doing the following using super glue: First, glue the inboard edge to the main wheel well top and allow it to set securely.

99

The Special Hobby 1/32nd scale F-80C kit is simply a reboxing of the previous Czech Model kit under a different label. The plastic is the same, but different decal options are provided. Again, Gil Hodges tackled the fit and alignment problems of the kit to build this nice model of "RAMBLIN'=RECK=TEW" that was flown by 1Lt. Robert Dewald of the 35th FBS when he shot down an IL-10 on June 27, 1950. Note the kill marking just below the framework of the windscreen. (Hodges)

Next, while bending the wing upward, glue the outer end of the part to the wing. Doing this on both sides will give the bottom wing some of the required dihedral. The wing tops can now be added, but don't forget to first drill out the locating holes in the bottom wing for the bomb pylons and underwing tip tanks!

At this point, the instructions can be followed to install the cockpit tub, nose wheel well, exhaust can, and then the fuselage halves can be glued together. I also recommend gluing the stabilizers in place, as these will serve as a check on fitting and aligning the wing. Also, don't forget to add some nose weight!

Even with all of the above adjustments, the fit of the wing assembly to the fuselage is problematic. The width of the fuselage tended to flatten out the wing and remove what dihedral had been set. I found that sanding each of the wing roots down allowed the wing to fit in place with the dihedral sustained and also result in a pretty good joint along the wing roots.

On the underside of the model, the fit is much worse, especially at the front. The wing simply needs to be glued in place while maintaining the dihedral, keeping the good fit along the wing roots, and assuring that the wings are level as compared to the tail planes. Ignore the steps on the bottom at the front and the back. The step in the front was too large to even be ground down. Instead, a "ramp" of epoxy putty was built up to smoothly transition the wing front to the rear of the nose wheel well. The same thing was needed at the rear junction of the

wing and fuselage, but to a lesser degree.

Another anomaly to be mentioned is the lack of a traditional axle on the main landing gear. The small nub meant to serve as an axle will only hold the wheel if it is glued to the brake drum on the wheel. I recommend drilling and pinning each gear leg to create an axle for each wheel. The fact that the brake drums are molded on the kit wheels instead of the gear legs means that if you want to flatten the tires by sanding them, there is only one spot to do it properly!

The nose gear, on the other hand, is more traditional in that it has an axle, although it is actually too long and has to be shortened. It also seems a tad on the flimsy side, and with weight added to the nose, I recommend shimming it with more thin sheet plastic or metal on the inside of the fork arm to strengthen it. After making the above adjustments, the kit can be finished out like any other kit.

If the above work seems a bit much, then the 1/32nd scale Czech Models F-80C isn't for you. However, if you're willing to stretch your proverbial modeling legs, challenge your building skills, and use some elbow grease, the end result can be very gratifying! Czech Models has provided an overall accurate and well detailed model of one of the more important Korean War fighter bombers. Just don't tackle it expecting a "shake-n-bake" experience, and you'll have a 1/32nd scale Shooting Star to proudly add to your collection!

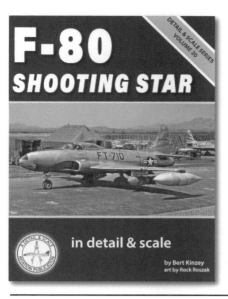

Get the digital edition!

The digital edition offers the same great content, with every high-resolution photograph expandable to full screen on your computer or mobile device. All at a much lower price. Visit our website at

www.detailandscale.com

to learn about all of our digital and print publications.

All Detail & Scale publications are available in both printed and digital (Apple and Amazon Kindle) formats. For current pricing, additional information,and ordering links, go to:

www.detailandscale.com

The Detail & Scale Series

ABOUT THE AUTHOR

Author Bert Kinzey graduated from Virginia Tech in 1968 with a degree in Business Administration. Upon graduation, he was commissioned a second lieutenant in the U. S. Army and was sent to the Army's Air Defense School at Fort Bliss, Texas.

During his eight years as an officer, Bert commanded a Hawk guided missile battery just south of the DMZ in Korea. Later he originated, wrote, and taught classes on the air threat, military air power, and air defense suppression at Fort Bliss.

It was during this time that he did his first writing. Bert was dissatisfied with the existing manuals and other materials available for his classes, because they were inaccurate and incomplete. As a result, he wrote his own reference books and other publications. Although he intended for these to be used only in his classes, they were soon placed on the Army's official publication list and distributed throughout the military.

In 1976, Bert resigned from active duty, but his reputation for being knowledgeable about all aspects of military air power soon led to his taking a civilian position as a subject matter expert on the air threat and world airpower with the Department of Defense. His primary responsibility was to develop a new program to teach the proper identification of both friendly and enemy aircraft, so as to insure the destruction of hostile aircraft and the safety of friendly aircraft. This was the first such program in the world to feature dynamic simulation. Bert has also flown with active, Reserve, and National Guard squadrons on training missions to observe the conduct and procedures of air-to-air and air-to-ground combat. As both an officer and a civilian, Bert often briefed military and political leaders of the United States and other nations on subjects related to air power, the air threat, and air defense.

While he was working for the Department of Defense, Bert started Detail & Scale, a part-time business to produce a new series of books on military aircraft. The Detail & Scale Series of publications was the first to focus on the many details of military aircraft to include cockpits, weapon systems, radars and avionics systems, differences between variants, airframe design, and much more. These books became so successful that Bert resigned from his position with the Department of Defense and began writing and producing books full time. Soon, other well-known aviation writers began writing books for the Detail & Scale Series, so Bert became both an author and an editor. Later Bert added aircraft carriers to the Detail & Scale Series, and he also began a second series called Colors & Markings. Each book in this series focused on a specific aircraft type and illustrated the paint schemes and markings of every unit that had flown that aircraft. Bert also produced a book for McGraw-Hill on the Gulf War entitled "The Fury of Desert Storm: The Air Campaign." In January 2002, Bert produced his one-hundredth aviation publication.

Bert has always taken many of the photographs that appear in his Detail & Scale Series publications, and he believes that whenever possible, it is best that the author take photos in order to precisely illustrate what is being discussed in the text and captions. His has also done photography for other books, magazine articles, websites, and for research and publicity that has been provided to clients. He owns one of the most extensive collections of aviation photographs in the world. Over the years, Bert has given numerous presentations and speeches about military air power, the air threat, military aviation history, and aircraft types, working these into his busy schedule of writing, editing, doing research, taking photographs, and consulting.

In June 2004, health issues caused Bert to retire from his work, and his two series of aviation books came to an end. But in 2011, the Detail & Scale website was created at www.detailandscale.com, and a Detail & Scale Facebook page was also begun. By the end of 2013, Bert had completed the first new title in the Detail & Scale Series in almost ten years, and more books were planned. Initially, these new titles were made available in digital formats, but in 2017, printed versions for titles in the Detail & Scale Series were also added. This new venture was made possible through a partnership with Rock Roszak.

Bert currently lives in Blacksburg, Virginia, with his wife Lynda. They have two children and five grandchildren.

ABOUT THE ILLUSTRATOR

The illustrator, Colonel Richard S. "Rock" Roszak, is the son of immigrants who came to America from a war-ravaged Europe. He grew up in Staunton, Virginia, and graduated from Virginia Tech in 1971 as a member of the Virginia Tech Corps of Cadets. He was commissioned into the United States Air Force where he earned his navigator wings and accumulated over 2,000 flying hours, mostly in B-52D/F/G and C-135 aircraft, over a 27-year active duty career. His staff tours included time as a special assistant to the Air Force Chief of Staff, liaison officer for strategic aircraft programs to the House and Senate Armed Services Committees, and as the Senior Technical Advisor to the Special Ambassador for assistance agreements to demilitarize strategic nuclear launch vehicles of the former Soviet Union. His final active duty tour was as the Commander, Air Force ROTC Detachment 875 at Virginia Tech, and during his tenure the detachment led the nation in earned scholarships and grew from the 36th to the 8th largest ROTC unit in the country.

After retiring from the Air Force in 1998, Rock spent 14 years on the staff of the Virginia Tech Corps of Cadets, returning to where he began his military career. During those years he established an alumni aviation gallery, which features his artwork of aircraft flown by cadet grads and highlights more than 80 years of military aviation history. An avid modeler in his younger years, he has been a digital artist for over twenty years and has illustrated several books in partnership with his friend, Bert Kinzey. In 2017, Rock's role at Detail & Scale expanded when he authored one book and co-authored another. He is art director and also responsible for publishing the books in both digital and print formats..

Rock currently lives in Blacksburg, Virginia, with his wife, Patty, two daughters, and six grandchildren.

Printed in Great Britain
by Amazon